LEADING THE

ASIAN AMERICAN ARTISTS OF THE OLDER GENERATION

PHOTOGRAPHIC PORTRAITS AND BIOGRAPHICAL SKETCHES BY IRENE POON

Irene Poon

2001

GORDON COLLEGE • WENHAM, MASSACHUSETTS • U.S.A. • 2001

ACKNOWLEDGEMENTS:

I am grateful to the 25 Asian American artists of the older generation whose support and generosity made this book possible. It was an honor for me to meet them, become acquainted with their wonderful and diverse work and hear how they came to be artists. I shall always treasure the experience and value the many new friendships.

In the beginning there were two people who were the catalysts for this book. Mark Johnson, director of the Fine Arts Gallery at San Francisco State University, gave me the opportunity to co-curate the landmark "With New Eyes" exhibition which opened my eyes in 1995. And, Dr. Whitney Chadwick, one of our art historians, supported me in the belief that I was the one to document photographically this older generation of artists.

As always, there are many others whose help was invaluable. I owe special thanks to So Kam Lee, curator of the exhibition at Gordon College concurrent with this book, Dr. Paul Karlstrom of the Archives of American Art, the collector Michael Brown for his help, Nanying Stella Wong for sharing her first experiences in art and Dr. Lorraine Dong for her valuable and informative advice about the historical background of my work.

A special acknowledgement goes to Rev. Philip Lee and family for their patronage, vision and believing in the worth of this book. My thanks also goes to the President of Gordon College, Dr. R. Judson Carlberg, as well as, Bruce Herman and David Goss for hosting and sponsoring the show at Gordon College. Also thanks to Craig Ing (Ing Design), for his wonderful design of this catalogue and book. To my friends, my colleagues at San Francisco State University and especially my family for their patience and understanding, I owe a debt of gratitude.

Last but most important, my husband Stan Andersen was there supporting me through the many ups and downs and was my valued sounding board and "live in editor."

— Irene Poon

Distributed by University of Washington Press, Seattle and London
ISBN 0-9707487-0-1

Design by: ING Design, Palo Alto, CA
This book is set in Gill Sans.

Printed in the United States • 2001

TABLE OF CONTENTS

PREFACE

My book **Leading The Way**, concerning Asian American artists from 1930 to 1970, evolved from the exhibition **"With New Eyes: Toward an Asian American Art History in the West"** that I co-curated in 1995 with Mark Johnson, Dawn Nakanishi and Diane Tani for the Art Department Gallery at San Francisco State University. In its five weeks the exhibition drew an unprecedented audience of nearly 5,000 people from the community at large as well as the campus. It received local, national and international coverage in the media as well as magazines like the *American Art Review* and *Asian Art News*. The exhibition revealed to me the potential strength of work created by artists of Asian descent.

When the exhibition came to a close, I found myself engulfed in sadness to part from the many beautiful works that were in the show. When I lamented my loss, one of our art historians, Dr. Whitney Chadwick, commented that someone should document some of these older artists before they're all gone. She then suggested that the someone should be me because I am both an accomplished photographer and Asian American. Who better, she said? At the time I told her no, I couldn't possibly because of the confines of my 40 hour a week job as the Slide Curator in the Art Department, my many family and community obligations and various other obstacles.

But the seed was planted. After many conversations with myself and my steadfast husband I decided that I cared enough about these artists and their place in history to give it my best try. Thus the book was launched. I began with a selection of some of the artists in the **"With New Eyes"** exhibition and branched out. This is by no means the definitive group of Asian American artists living today, but my personal choices. I was saddened to learn of the passing of three of those I chose even as the book began to be realized.

Each photographic session I had with these artists yielded memories, impressions and lessons that I will never forget. I never dreamt that I would actually meet Dong Kingman or Jade Snow Wong who were role models for me when I was a child growing up in San Francisco's Chinatown. It was a revelation for me to learn that the artist George Tsutakawa was a major figure in a circle that included Morris Graves and Mark Tobey; that Bernice Bing, George Miyasaki and Arthur Okamura were part of the Abstract Expressionists on the West Coast; and that Tyrus Wong was the artist responsible for the inspirational paintings that created **"Bambi"** for the Disney Studios. As I learned more about these artists, I wondered why I had never seen their names in the art history books when I was in school earning my degrees in art and photography. I would like my book to prove that there are more Asian American artists creating wonderful work meriting recognition than Yasuo Kuniyoshi and Isamu Noguchi, the two distinguished artists mentioned in the modern art history books.

This book is dedicated to acknowledging some of the older Asian American artists who led the way with their artwork in the decades of the 30s through the 60s. May their work help rewrite American art history.

Irene Poon
2001

INTRODUCTION — IMAGING THE PAST

Irene Poon is embarked upon an historic recovery mission. Her photographs, the subject of this book and exhibition, are in the vanguard of what amounts to an enfranchising project directed at the Asian American art community. The enterprise has great significance for Asian Pacific American studies and the history of art in America, and it provides further insight into just what it means to be an American. Somewhat slowly we have come to understand that there is no single, unitary narrative reaching back to Europe, Plymouth Rock and the Boston Tea Party that can describe the American experience. The great adventure now is to retrieve the many missing or ignored elements, group and individual, of the mosaic. And that is the project in which Poon's sensitive portraits of senior Asian American artists from California, Hawaii, Washington State and New York City participate.

Poon has been involved in the retrieval of Asian American art and artists practically from the beginning of when scholars and a few collectors began to take notice. She was part of the curatorial team that organized the pioneering exhibition *With New Eyes: Toward an Asian American Art History in the West* mounted at San Francisco State University in 1995. Although I had known her and her professor husband Stan Andersen almost twenty years, it was then that I met her in connection with our shared interest in this subject. I myself had recently directed a project to document for the national collections Asian American artists in the Pacific Northwest. The Northwest Asian American Artist Project was inspired by a video interview conducted in 1987 with Seattle sculptor George Tsutakawa as part of the Archives of American Art oral history program. The opportunity one year later to follow Tsutakawa to Japan to record on video tape the installation of a piece commissioned by his ancestral home, Fukuyama, broadened the scope of my project to address issues of artistic expression based on two (actually more) cultures. A major theme that emerged from the first interview was the question of creative identity among artists such as Tsutakawa and other Asian Americans of his generation. It soon became evident that an important part of their stories was a struggle to reconcile the powerful emotional influence of their cultural "homeland" (whether or not they were born there) with the creative energy and experimental openness of the United States. A further conflict arose between a perceived obligation to serve the interests of ethnic identity and the "agency" involved in artistic independence, a hallmark of modernist art.

The results of this project appeared in a directory published in *They Painted From Their Hearts: Pioneer Asian American Artists*, organized by Mayumi Tsutakawa (George's daughter), also in 1995, for Seattle's Wing Luke Asian Museum. Shortly thereafter these two enterprises converged in a collaboration between San Francisco State University and the Smithsonian Institution Archives of American Art. Irene Poon is also involved in the ambitious *California Asian American Artists Biographical Survey*, the outcome of which will be a book presenting the documentation of one thousand artists working in California between 1840 and 1965. Poon's colleague at San Francisco State, gallery director Mark Johnson and I serve as co-editors of the publication which is scheduled to appear in 2004. Her photographs will no doubt provide the portraits accompanying entries for some of the leading artists in the survey.

Among Poon's twenty-five subjects are at least three who have subsequently passed away, including George Tsutakawa, Dong Kingman and Bernice Bing. Fortunately, they have been documented in interviews and will continue to be through papers deposited at the Smithsonian or elsewhere. This is the main goal in the ongoing enterprise in which Poon and others of us are engaged. This, however, applies to the better known artists. In Poon's portfolio only a few names, perhaps three or four, are familiar outside the Asian American communities. Even art historians would be hard pressed to name more than a handful. The others have been effectively submerged from an historical perspective. Poon's revealing portraits, intelligently located in settings that communicate about the subjects, preserve the images of individuals whose art world presence we seek to secure for history. Ruth Asawa, for example, is shown at home with her famous clay masks. James Leong stands in front of his 1952 *One Hundred Years: History of the Chinese in America* mural now preserved, through Poon's efforts, at the Chinese Historical Society of America and Chinese American National Museum in San Francisco.

Poon's work represents the most comprehensive effort to compile a visual portrait of the Asian American artist community. Her photographs richly complement and enhance the other forms of documentation being gathered. I feel privileged to have this opportunity to join her in this critical endeavor.

Paul J. Karlstrom
West Coast Regional Director
Smithsonian Institution Archives of American Art
7 October 2000 / San Francisco

FOREWORD

Irene Poon's book about 25 Asian American artists she has known and photographed during her own distinguished career pays tribute to those who have led the way into American art history. She has compiled a book about the "pioneers" she found to emulate when she began creating images of the world around her, both within and beyond her own Chinatown San Francisco.

I speak gratefully for all of us she devotedly portrays. We are artists heretofore not well known. She introduces us to the American art public.

Like all artists we need critical understanding. Being an artist herself, she wants to see how these earlier American artists with Asian roots did their work and then through her photographs to portray them as still being spiritually capable of doing it. She is no "art historian," she claims, but she's certainly a true recorder of lives given to art. Both her words and her photographs demonstrate how art is made.

I'm the one chosen to write a foreword to Leading the Way, I suppose, because my career goes back well into the beginnings of modern Asian American art. But this is not to say we are all alike, that one story fits all. Irene Poon shows the different paths we've taken into the company of American artists. Her book joins together many personalities and life stories, but each remains a separate piece of the whole weave, a different path.

Leading the Way gains its interest from this fact. It could also be titled Leading Many Ways.

My own career began about 50 years before Irene Poon's, when I danced at 4 years old in my Grandma and Dad's Chinese restaurant "Hing Sing Low" in Oakland for coins tossed on the dance floor. The Wong family as early as that aspired to fame. We tried the new art of movie-making too (as did another Wong named Anna May a bit later). My mom, Violet Jung Wong, joined her sister-in-law the writer and singer Marion Hong in making a silent movie in Milpitas about an overseas Grandma and her son who went to China to find him a wife. Its title was "The Curse of Kwan Kung." I was the baby of the film's happy ending that lifted the curse. The grownups "led the way" into such new paths in order to escape working forever in a Chinese restaurant—vital as restaurants such as "Hing Sing Low" were both for nourishment and for jobs. We young ones followed.

So, you see, Asian artists, singers, performers young and old have been around all along, even if they had to stir-fry chow mein to make a living!

Of course we were children of the times. Grandma Chan See went to Oakland and started the restaurant there because of the great Earthquake and Fire of 1906. Nature in eruption gave her and her family the chance to leave their Chinatown Ghetto home, along with other Americans who rode the ferryboat to Oakland. Eva Fong Chan, an artist my mother knew in the old Oakland family days—they played tennis together—passed on to me a photo my Mom had given her when I was a baby. It showed Mom, Dad and myself, she in a stylish Chinese garment, he in his American dark suit, and I in a fluffy American dress sitting on his lap. It was a time capsule of Chinese American family in transition to the modern ways.

Natural and social forces together were totally changing the people of this family resolutely facing the future and the artists of various American worlds too.

I remember taking part in San Francisco's first outdoor art shows. The artists used the old City of Paris Department Store as their base, daily installing their art works for display at Union Square. I brushed Chinese proverbs as giveaways to the viewers, and donated to the cause of that time a watercolor I painted of my two younger sisters in Chinese jackets and trousers chopsticking rice from their bowls into their mouths. I think the key event that day was "The Rice Bowl." My watercolor was raffled off to an enthusiastic crowd and featured in American newspapers.

I very much liked the way that painting and event brought me my first significant recognition. We Asian American artists had as much to contribute to American art history as anyone, each in our own way. My subject, sisters eating, was the stamp of my talent being appreciated.

Irene Poon's book is like that to me now more than a half century later. It invites all who love art to enjoy Asian American art with the rest. And it shows how and why this art comes into being.

Nanying Stella Wong
Berkeley, California
September 2000

HISTORICAL ESSAY —

THE WAY ASIAN AMERICANS CAME AND SURVIVED

When Ferdinand Magellan "discovered" some islands in 1521 that were later named the Philippine Islands, he claimed them for Spain and the Catholic Church. The indigenous people were subsequently enslaved for the Spanish galleon trade that operated between Manila and Acapulco. Many jumped ship and escaped as soon as the ships docked on the western shores of America. Today, their descendants are known as Filipino Cajuns, 10th generation Filipinos of mixed heritage. Thus begins the earliest record of Asians arriving in the United States during the 16th century.

The Chinese and Indians had the next earliest recording of Asian arrival in the United States. In 1785, a ship landed in Baltimore, Maryland, with thirty-two Indian sailors and three Chinese seamen. By the late 1840s to early 1850s, California experienced the biggest increase in its Chinese population (about 25,000 in 1851; 11.2% of the state's total population) and the Chinese became the largest Asian ethnic group in America. The rise of the Chinese amidst a poor economy made them scapegoats for the country's woes. Many were driven out of town or killed. The unemployed declared side-by-side with politicians that "The Chinese must go!" The anti-Chinese movement climaxed with the infamous 1882 Chinese Exclusion Act that banned Chinese from naturalization. More importantly, it banned Chinese skilled and unskilled laborers from entering the United States for ten years. Subsequent exclusion acts extended the ten years until it was extended indefinitely in 1904. Chinese immigration was reduced drastically, with only the exempt classes of merchants, students, diplomats and tourists permitted to enter.

When the economy improved, the demand for cheap labor turned America's eyes towards Japan because the Chinese Exclusion Acts eliminated Chinese as a source of cheap labor. Japanese arrivals to America began as early as the 1860s, and grew rapidly in the 1890s as a result of the anti-Chinese movement. However, anti-Japanese sentiments rose soon as Americans also considered them to be "dangerous" economic competitors and unassimilable aliens who were loyal only to a Japanese emperor gaining more and more military power. By 1905, groups like the Asiatic Exclusion League began to advocate Japanese exclusion. In 1908, Japan and the United States reached a Gentlemen's Agreement, whereby Japan voluntarily withheld passports issued to skilled or unskilled laborers going to America. This was later extended in 1921 to include picture brides who came to America to marry Japanese bachelors. As a consequence, Japanese immigration also suffered a major decline.

Of special note is the Korean case. The Hawaii Sugar Planters Association recruited Korean workers in the early 1900s, but the tactic of hiring Korean laborers was stopped by the Japanese emperor when Japan formally annexed Korea in 1910 and named it Chosen. Koreans were Japanese subjects and recognized as "Japanese" by the United States government, which meant all domestic laws that applied to the Japanese applied equally to the Koreans.

The Hawaii Sugar Planters Association also went to the Philippines to recruit cheap labor in the early 1900s. By this time, the Philippines had become a U.S. territory when the Philippine-American War (1898-1900) ended with America "purchasing" the Islands for $20 million. As they were U.S. nationals, it was relatively easier for Filipinos to travel to the United States, and thus they were a more convenient source of recruitment.

In addition, the 1903 Pensionado Act gave U.S. scholarships to Filipino students to study in America. By the 1930s, the Filipino population had increased 66% in Hawaii and 88% on the mainland. Their visibility did not help when the country's economy once again fell. Similar to what had happened to the Chinese and Japanese, Americans now saw Filipinos as dangerous and stealing their jobs. They wanted Filipino exclusion. However, this was unacceptable because the Philippines was a U.S. territory with loyalty to the United States. A compromise to exclusion was the passage of the 1934 Tydings-McDuffie Independence Act, which made the Islands a commonwealth nation for ten years and restricted their immigration to a quota of fifty per year. This victory for the anti-Filipino movement led to the decline of yet another Asian group in America.

World War II marked a turning point for Asian American history. When the United States declared war against Japan on December 8, 1941, one day after Japan bombed Honolulu, the government's attitudes toward the various Asian groups changed. No longer viewed as a devious, infiltrating "Yellow Peril," Chinese were now staunch supporters of democracy. China was an ally fighting against Japan. In order to silence Japanese war propaganda that told the world how America treated its ally by excluding Chinese, President Franklin D. Roosevelt signed the Repeal of the Chinese Exclusion Acts on December 17, 1943. The Repeal permitted Chinese to naturalize for U.S. citizenship and implemented an annual immigration quota system of 100 Koreans, 105 Chinese and 185 Japanese. This ended sixty-one years of exclusion.

While the nation was patting its back for ending one chapter of racism, it was deep in the midst of another chapter of racism. Japan was now the new Yellow Peril. On February 19, 1942, President Franklin signed Executive Order 9066 that led to the internment of Japanese American citizens on the West Coast. Accused of being spies, and in the name of national security and military necessity, approximately 120,000 people of Japanese ancestry were forced to ten internment camps where they were incarcerated without trial for the next three years. They had to leave their homes, jobs and schools to live under barren conditions. Seventy thousand were U.S. citizens whose constitutional rights were totally ignored. Those who were not citizens, could not be citizens because of the law. An estimated 1,800 died in the camps, mostly of natural causes aggravated by the imprisonment. One died after being shot by a guard. The guard was fined one dollar for the unauthorized use of a U.S. property, the bullet. The final cost to the government for putting away a group of innocent people found guilty purely for their ethnicity, was $248+ million.

Guilty until proven innocent, the Japanese Americans had to wait until February 1943, when the Secretary of War implemented a controversial loyalty oath that was a feeble attempt at proving loyalty or disloyalty. Nevertheless, this loyalty oath provided a mechanism for some Japanese Americans to serve as loyal soldiers in the U.S. Army. Ironically, while fighting and dying for the United States to liberate Europeans from Hitler and Mussolini, those soldiers had to bear the imprisonment of their families in American camps. Known as the 100/442, they nonetheless became the most decorated group of World War II with over 5,900 medals and commendations. Yet, when they returned to their hometowns after the war, some were welcomed with guns pointed towards them and told to leave.

Technically "Japanese," the Koreans would have had to endure the same conditions. But their Korean Independence Movement, which heretofore had been ignored by the United States, was now recognized as an anti-Japanese movement. Hence, in 1942, Koreans were no longer required to register as enemy aliens. They were exempt from internment; some who enlisted in the military were assigned to the 100/442.

Other than the Japanese, all Asian American communities were actively engaged in anti-Japanese activities to liberate their ancestral countries from Japanese occupation. This also meant supporting America's entry in the war. Chinese, Koreans and Filipinos patriotically joined the military to serve the United States, with the Japanese Americans doing it for different reasons. As for the Filipinos, the struggle was not just against Japanese occupation, but also American occupation. On July 4, 1946, President Harry S. Truman "proclaimed" independence for the Philippines.

The friendly relationship with the Chinese and Koreans did not last long after the end of World War II. With America's entry into the Cold War, communism was the country's biggest enemy. China was the Yellow Peril again. Along with Russian Americans, Chinese and Korean Americans had to undergo the same suspicion and allegations that the Japanese Americans did before World War II. The fear of being put in camps was still fresh in everyone's minds. During the Cold War period, Chinese and Korean Americans did their best to prove that they were loyal Americans and not communists.

Meanwhile, the Japanese Americans who were released from the camps underwent what some call "social amnesia." They did not want their descendants to grow up hating America, so they kept quiet and did not talk about the camps. They continued with their lives and raised their families to be all-American. It was not until 1952, that the government finally allowed the Japanese and Koreans their naturalization rights.

America's immigration law had its biggest change in 1965. All previous quotas were eliminated and each country was now allotted an annual quota of 20,000. With this huge jump from the first Filipino quota of fifty, the Asian American population began to grow in earnest. Post World War II war brides and soldier brides had begun the process of bringing more Asian women into this country, but with the 1965 immigration act, the Asian American bachelor society of the early days saw its decline and death. Families were reunited and created, and a diverse Asian American citizenry was born in the United States. Now known as Asian Pacific Islander Americans, they are approximately 4% of the total U.S. population.

Much hard work and struggle went into the making of this population who came and won due respect. Nevertheless, despite their many success stories, they are still plagued with the stereotypes of "yellow peril" and "model minority" even as they enter the 21st century. Irene Poon's book shows that artists of Asian American communities did their significant part in their communities' full arrival in U.S. society.

Lorraine Dong, Ph.D.,
Professor of Asian American Studies
San Francisco State University
November 2000

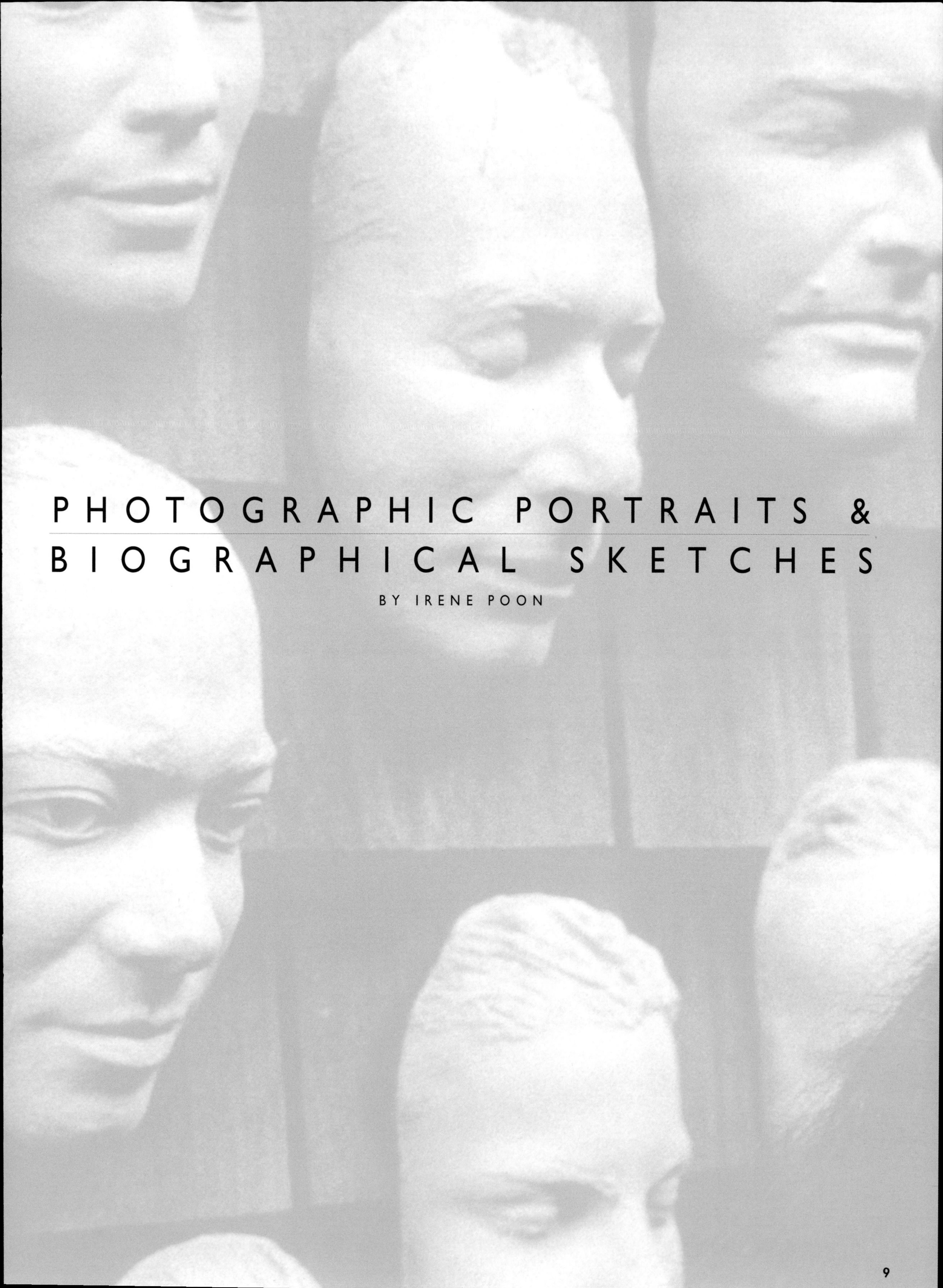

PHOTOGRAPHIC PORTRAITS &
BIOGRAPHICAL SKETCHES

BY IRENE POON

RUTH ASAWA
(born 1926)

Ruth Asawa grew up in the small farming community of Norwalk, California, near Los Angeles where her family ran a truck farm. Ruth attended public schools in the Norwalk area and was encouraged early in art by one of her teachers. Ruth dreamed of attending the Chouinard Art Institute or the Otis Art Institute in Los Angeles. But this was not to be as the onset of World War II and Executive Order 9066 disrupted the lives of Japanese inhabitants on the west coast.

Ruth finished high school at the internment camp at Rohwer, Arkansas. She was qualified to apply for college admission to any school not on the west coast, and she was admitted to Milwaukee State Teachers College in 1943. She studied drawing, painting, printmaking, ceramics and jewelry. Ruth was influenced by Howard Thomas, who taught during the summers at the famous Black Mountain College. After leaving Milwaukee Ruth made the decision to apply to Black Mountain College in the North Carolina countryside since anti-Japanese sentiments would keep her from being a public school teacher.

The three years Ruth spent at Black Mountain College transformed her life. She was enveloped in the community of the place and challenged by the teachings of Josef Albers and the architect Buckminster Fuller. Ruth would later apply Fuller's message of going forth and finding one's own ways to creativity in pursuit of her own identity as an artist and her own priorities in sharing the world of art in the public schools.

In 1949, Ruth married her fellow Black Mountain student, Albert Lanier, and moved to San Francisco. Ruth created her home-studio while Albert established his architectural practice. As their family grew, the lessons and life style from the Black Mountain days were reflected in the Asawa-Lanier home where art was a normal part of the home and the everyday chores. Ruth pictured herself a painter since her training had been in color, design and watercolors; but her own inquisitive experiments with wire changed all that. She "drew" with wire, beginning with simple basket shapes which evolved and multiplied into many other shapes and volumes. She has said, "I like wire because it's so transparent. You can see right through it and it makes shadows and it defines the sculpture better than the sculpture itself when you get a shadow on it. And I like the quality of the transparency. It's sort of like insect wings and bubbles—you know, soap bubbles. I like the lightness and the kind of fragility of it and I'm pleased with how it looks."*

Ruth went on to building fountains for public places such as the one for the Grand Hyatt in San Francisco where she used the "baker's clay" method with school children helping in the creation of the images which were cast in bronze for the fountain. One of the recent sculptures Ruth completed was the bronze Japanese American Internment Memorial dedicated in 1994 at the Federal Building in the city of San Jose. Ruth has garnered many awards for her work as well as serving on many civic committees. She is busy as ever with her artwork and being the outspoken champion of the arts as a way to enrich the lives of children in the public schools as well as the larger community.

* Excerpted from television interview for With New Eyes, an exhibition of 1995 featured in Sunday on 7, KGO -TV San Francisco

BERNICE BING
(1936 - 1998)

Bernice Bing or "Bingo" as she was fondly called by her friends was born in San Francisco in 1936. Her childhood was chaotic after the death of her mother when Bing was only 6 years old. She never knew her father. She was shuffled through various foster homes and shelters though she did spend some time with her grandmother.

"As a child, I was isolated. I did a lot of drawing on my own. I had a great difficulty in communicating with my grandmother. She was from a very strict old school. She had bound feet and so she had a lot of anger. And I remember doing a lot of drawing and that was the only thing she praised—when I did a drawing or something. So that sort of encouraged me and it was a nice kind of communication."

In high school, Bing was very artistic but not academically inclined. She attended Oakland Technical High School and did a lot of art there resulting in a scholarship to either attend the Chounaird Art School in Los Angeles or the California College of Arts and Crafts in Oakland. She chose Arts and Crafts and was aided financially by public welfare and individuals who provided her a small stipend for school. She began as an advertising major. "I was actually looking for a vocation that would be steady and paid well. I had no idea I was going to be a poor artist."

While she was at Arts and Crafts, a single figure stood out most vividly in her memory. "Here's this very mysterious Asian man in black robes, Zen robes, he didn't speak much English but I did take some classes with him. I knew nothing about Chinese culture, Asian culture, or religion or philosophy. That certainly wasn't the main emphasis in art school during that time. We had Western art history." This man in black was the Zen master, Saburo Hasegawa. He was brought to teach at Arts and Crafts by Allan Watts, and introduced Zen and Eastern thought as well as the Existential writers.

Bing was influenced by "Camus and Sartre and the Existential writers during that time, and with the combination of the intriguing Zen and Existentialism. I began to think about it, and more in depth about art generally, I was getting tired of doing commercial art because it was a lot of repetition." So Bing started investigating the fine arts. This was a time of "tremendous amount of energy and good feeling, things happening at Arts and Crafts during that time. Oliveira was teaching there and Diebenkorn was a young man just beginning to gain recognition and he was very much an influence on me going into painting." Then a disagreement between the faculty and administration led to an exodus from Arts and Crafts of faculty as well as students to the California School of Fine Arts, now the San Francisco Art Institute.

In the Fall of 1958, Bing transferred to the School of Fine Arts. There she studied with Elmer Bischoff, a "very articulate person during that time with Joan Brown, Manuel Neri and Al Light. There was a lot going on. We were all buddies, hung out together and drank together. Jay de Feo and Wally Hedrick were all seniors and Bill Brown, all those guys were great. It was an exciting time and I was so naïve and bright eyed and taking everything in. I went into abstraction. I responded to that more than I did figurative art." She went on to study with the painter Frank Lobdell during her graduate years.

After graduation, Bing moved to the Napa countryside where she was the caretaker at the Mayacamas Vineyards. She "dropped out of the scene." But she felt she did "some very inspirational work." Bing eventually had to go back to San Francisco for employment. There she helped start the neighborhood arts program in the Chinatown and Northbeach communities. She had the facility to organize projects, like workshops and getting people together and make them happen. She was also the director of the South of Market Cultural Center (SOMAR) for a time.

In 1984, Bing visited China for the first time. There she went to the Beijing Academy of Art where she "had a crash course in Chinese calligraphy and in Chinese painting. It wasn't very long but just that little bit of experience was quite grand." She became interested in the ideograms and did a lot of research. "I did a lot of calligraphy, copying a lot of calligraphy. I was already working pretty much in the abstract mode so I sort of incorporated calligraphy into my images. It was very exciting at that time putting all these ideas together. In a roundabout way I was able to integrate my ethnicity into my art."

After her return from China, Bing moved from San Francisco back to the country, to Philo, a small town in Mendocino County, north California. She supported herself waitressing, cooking, and as a counselor at a youth rehabilitation center. She continued to paint in a small outdoor studio. "I don't feel isolated," she told me then. "I like the solitude. It feels right."

Bernice Bing passed on in 1998. A painting from the Napa country days, "Mayacamas # 6," was acquired by the Fine Arts Museums of San Francisco for their American collection in March of 2000.

— IPA interview with Bernice Bing 1997

WAH MING CHANG
(born 1917)

Wah Ming Chang was born in Honolulu and grew up in San Francisco where his parents operated a tearoom. The Ho Ho Tearoom was a gathering place for artists, writers, musicians and actors. Wah was immersed in art early in life. His mother was an accomplished commercial artist, actress and costume designer, and his father was a designer of Christmas cards as well as the cook in the tearoom.

Wah was never discouraged from being creative. He began producing drawings when he was only two years old. He was befriended by the artist Blanding Sloan, a tearoom regular. Sloan taught Wah the art of making etchings, building puppets and creating stage sets. Soon, just 8 years old, Wah was exhibiting his work in galleries. Sloan would not only be a mentor to Wah but his "family" after his mother died and his father went on a solo journey when Wah was 11. Under Sloan and his wife's wing, Wah the child prodigy blossomed into a many faceted artist. There was nothing he couldn't do.

In 1939, Wah went to work at the Walt Disney Studios making articulated models for "Bambi" and "Fantasia" and "…models, and clocks and toys that were designs for 'Pinocchio'." He recalls, "It was a good place to work, but it was extremely low paying. I was paid $20 a week at Disney." This work was interrupted in 1940 when Wah was stricken with polio and spent a year in a sanitarium to recover. He then went to work for the George Pal Studios doing puppetoons and some training films for the military.

Wah quit working for the studios and opened his own East-West Studios, and produced an award winning film with Blanding Sloan called "The Way of Peace" for the Lutheran Church. Then Wah and a friend, Gene Warren, went into business to produce and design toys. Wah made the first Barbie doll model as well as masks for the ballet sequence in the film "The King And I," and the familiar Pillsbury Doughboy.

In the 50s and 60s, Wah and Warren won two Academy Awards for special effects for the films "The Time Machine" and "Tom Thumb." This was only the beginning of Wah's long and illustrious career as the master of special effects. In the 60s, Wah began his association with the "Star Trek" television series, creating many of its special effects beaming us further into space. He also made many commercials before turning to educational and environmental causes and films with his late wife. At this time, Wah makes many bronze sculptures of animals.

In January of 2000, the Monterey Museum of Art honored Wah with a retrospective exhibition "The Imaginative World of Wah Ming Chang" attended by legions of friends and admirers of his creative genius. Today, Wah lives quietly on the Carmel coast in the house he designed and built.

— IPA interview with Wah Ming Chang 1998

BENJAMEN CHINN
(born 1921)

Benjamen Chinn came from a family of 12 children. He was born in San Francisco in 1921. The family home was on Commercial Street in Chinatown. Chinn attended a Methodist kindergarten before going to public schools.

Chinn's interest in photography began as a hobby when he was in middle school. His first teacher was one of his brothers. Chinn was fascinated "…just to see the image come up in the solution, that's the thing that's surprising and amazing…" He was the school photographer through each phase of his education. He recalls that in a high school botany class, he had a little pocket folding camera that he put "…on top of the microscope, taking pictures of experiments." The teacher "thought I was playing around…so she made me stay after school. But by the end of the semester, I had these six enlargements—8x10 enlargements of what I saw through the microscope. She reversed herself and gave me an 'A' in the class."

During World War II, Chinn served in the U.S. Army Air Corps as an aerial photographer in Hawaii. His favorite plane for missions was a "B26 converted bomber, two engines, with no armament, no bombs, just the gas tank and camera."

After his discharge from the Army in 1946, Chinn enrolled at the California School of Fine Arts (now the San Francisco Art Institute) to study photography in the first class taught by Ansel Adams, founder of the program. The other primary instructor was Minor White. During this time, many lecturers like Imogen Cunningham, Ruth Bernhard, Lisette Model, Dorothea Lange also taught there. Chinn had his own darkroom and didn't mix with the other students. He was admired for his excellent printing.

Besides photography, Chinn took classes in painting and sculpture. His painting instructors were Dorr Bothwell and Richard Diebenkorn, both of whom Chinn regarded as great teachers. In 1949, Chinn went to Paris to study art at the L'Acadieme Juliane. One of his teachers there was the sculptor Alberto Giacometti. Chinn vividly recalls him. "He's very strict. You see his very skinny, emaciated figures. But when you study with him he's completely realistic. He wouldn't allow anything. You model with clay and he'll come and measure with a caliper the model and your model." Chinn also went to the Lachaise School and the Sorbonne to study geography and philosophy.

After his sojourn in Paris, he was first employed as assistant to the chief engineer at the U.S. Pipe and Steel Company. In 1953, Chinn got a job with the Department of Defense as Chief of Photographic Services with the U.S. 6th Army, then as Chief of Training Aids Division until his retirement in 1984.

Chinn's photographic work was shown in the group exhibition "Perception" at the California Palace of the Legion of Honor in San Francisco, and most recently (1998) in an exhibition celebrating the 50th anniversary of Ansel Adams first class in photography. His work was included in the exhibition and book *An American Century of Photography: From Dry-Plate to Digital, the Hallmark Photographic Collection* 1995.

Benjamen Chinn has said "I never consider myself an artist, I still don't. I've always been pretty much of a loner." He has hitchhiked alone all over Israel, France and several times to Mexico to live with the Indians. He has taken aerial photographs from a hot air balloon in New Mexico. Today, Chinn still lives on Commercial Street in San Francisco Chinatown and can be seen practicing what he has taught: to "walk down the sidewalk and see things as you walk by. Take your time and just meander around."

— IPA interview with Benjamen Chinn 1998

TANEYUKI DAN HARADA
(born 1923)

Taneyuki Dan Harada was introduced to art in 1942 when his family was interned at the Tanforan Assembly Center in California. Harada was swept up in the excitement of an art school created by Chiura Obata and Matsusaburo Hibi at the Center. He recalls the place as "teeming with young people... a lot of teachers like Miné Okubo, Frank Taira and others...and there was so many students the place was really packed everyday...it was a very exciting place and that was [my] first... connection with art."

When his family was moved to the Topaz Internment Camp in Utah, Harada joined the art school where Hibi, Obata and Byron Tsuzuki taught painting. He studied with Hibi and came to consider him the mentor who taught him everything. This period of study ended when Harada was sent to the Leapp Isolation Center in Arizona for being a disloyal troublemaker. He was there from July to December of 1943 before being sent to the Tule Lake Segregation Center. He no longer had Hibi to guide him. He went to the art school at Tule Lake and joined a group of older students experimenting in the styles of Van Gogh, Renoir and others. Harada had his first one-man show in the ironing room of Block 5 in 1945.

It was at Tule Lake that he painted *The Barracks, Topaz* from a sketch he had made at Topaz. Harada's inspiration was the work of Albert Pinkham Ryder whose colors were "dreary, dark and atmospheric." He wanted to depict the barracks as "symbols of incarceration."

After his release, Harada attended the College of Arts and Crafts in Oakland from 1947 to 1949, studying commercial design and illustration. He worked at the Simmons Mattress Company and as a strawberry and grape picker and a gardener's helper to make a living. He kept painting and exhibited his work in group shows during the late 1940s. In the 1950s Harada became a computer programmer for the Federal Government, retiring in late 1980.

Harada now says, "I really want to be able to paint like an innocent child, direct, pure color...I just want to enjoy my life...I just want to enjoy painting..."

— IPA interview with Taneyuki Dan Harada 1998

DALE JOE
(born 1928)

Dale Joe was born in San Bernardino, California in 1928. He recalls, "I more or less have always been interested in art and I took courses from different people all through my life as a teenager. I studied under Richards Ruben, a California based person, and I really enjoyed it very much, but I never thought of it as a profession or not a thing to do in life until I went to the University of California at Berkeley."

In the early 1950s, Joe was a creative writing and English literature major at the University of California, where he received his B.A. He never finished his M.A. in this field because he was not allowed to work in his area of interest. "I thought this was the most depressing thing so I started taking courses in art and got involved. I studied under Felix Ruvulo and Miné Okubo. I was really very much influenced and they urged me to go on with work in the visual arts which I'd been attracted to before but never thought of throwing my entire being into."

Joe studied painting and printmaking with Ruvulo and Leon Goldin and attended classes and lectures by Richards Ruben, Sybil Moholy-Nagy, Miné Okubo and Claire Falkenstein. During this period, he also attended the California College of Arts and Crafts in Oakland. Joe began entering his work in competitions such as the San Francisco Art Association's Annual Exhibition held at the San Francisco Museum of Art, now the San Francisco Museum of Modern Art. This was around 1951-52. He was very successful. "I won first prize in the print and drawing competition. I won in the watercolor and I got into the oil painting. I didn't win first prize in oils which was the big thing to do." These prizes gained Joe instant recognition. Joe designed sets for the Inter-players in San Francisco for their production of "Dear Judas" by Robinson Jeffers as well as August Strindberg's "Miss Julie." Joe recalls, "The theater reviewers noticed the sets utilizing banners in the splash paint technique more than the play 'Miss Julie.'"

In 1953, Joe moved to New York City after he received a John Hay Whitney Fellowship Award to study there. "I was going to become an assistant to Bradley Walker Tomlin because of my admiration for his calligraphic approach to painting. He and I wrote to each other and we got along very well. I thought I would assist him at his studio, but a month before I arrived he died. And so I was without a plan when I came here but that really didn't matter, so I sort of browsed around and introduced myself to a lot of people." These people included Jack Tworkov, Allan Kaprow and Wolf Kahn.

Joe's change of plans involved an independent study of the handwriting of western authors at the Pierpont Morgan Library as well as studying calligraphy with Master Wang in his studio at Carnegie Hall.

In 1954, Joe had his first big show at the Urban Gallery in New York City. The Gallery exhibited the work of young artists like Allan Kaprow, Leon Golub and Felix Pasilis. Joe was affiliated with the Urban Gallery until 1955 when the gallery closed. At this same time, Joe also had many exhibitions at the Mi Chou Gallery which featured modern paintings by Asian American and native Asian artists like Noriko Yamamoto, Bernice Bing and Chen Chi Kwan. Joe had combined Action Painting, Abstract Expressionism and the Direct Inkwriting of the Asian avant-garde into his work.

In 1956-57, Joe was awarded a Fulbright Fellowship to study in France. There he studied the drawings of Degas as well as the Lascaux Cave paintings. Joe returned to the United States in 1958. Upon his return, his work was chosen for a national traveling exhibition of Fulbright artists at the Smithsonian Institute in Washington, D.C. Then in 1960, his paintings were chosen for the "Young America" exhibition at the Whitney Museum. And during this period, he designed a piece for the Steuben Glass Company called "Poetry in Crystal."

In the 70s, Joe's fortune as a painter plateaued due to the closure of the Mi Chou gallery and the new art movements that replaced Abstract Expressionism. Among these movements was Pop Art. Joe "understood the whole idea of Pop Art but I didn't feel that I should do it merely because it was something everyone was doing." Joe knew Andy Warhol, one of Pop Art's leading figures. "Andy Warhol made this sort of playpen on 47th Street, the first factory. We all went there and everybody had a good time. We sort of disrespected him and I always felt he was a commercial artist. Andy gave us a lot of things that were really good. He gave us the freedom to work with materials that were put down by the old guard. He said it was okay to work with a lot of situations that were a very commercial art kind of thing." But with the decline of interest in his work, Joe was forced to make a living at something other than his art.

He chose to work as a freelance Home Projects designer for magazines such as "Family Circle," "Woman's Day" and "McCalls." His friend Bob Anderson of "Family Circle" offered him the chance to work full time but Joe turned him down since it would take away time and energy from his paintings. Joe worked for the magazines for about 15 years. "I wouldn't have done it unless it was fun."

Today, Dale Joe's work has gained renewed interest due to recent exhibitions like the big "Asian Traditions/Modern Abstraction" show at Rutgers University in 1997 which traveled through 1998, and the 1999 retrospective of his work at the University of Iowa Museum of Art.

— IPA interview with Dale Joe 1998

DIANA KAN
(born 1926)

Diana Kan's work embodies East meeting West. She was born in Hong Kong in 1926, the seventh in a family of nine children, and was immersed in art at an early age. Her father was a prominent calligrapher and seal carver, her mother a noted writer. She learned the discipline of traditional Chinese calligraphy, considered the foundation for brush painting, from her father. From her mother and other philosophic writers she learned the craft of writing.

Kan was a child prodigy who declared that she would paint better than God. She had her first painting exhibition when she was 9 years old at the National Academy of Fine Arts in Shanghai, and published her first poetry at age 12. And at the age of 21 she was the chosen disciple of the prodigious artist Chang Dai-chien whom many consider the Picasso of China. Kan studied with Master Chang for forty years learning to copy the ancient masters and honing her skills with the brush. Duplicating the work of the masters was standard practice in the teaching of the fundamentals of calligraphy and painting. The highest praise an aspiring painter could have is that their work was indistinguishable from the masters.

Kan was a diligent pupil of exceptional talent. She quickly mastered control of the brush and ink and went on to the technique of splash ink painting or Po Mo which she learned from Chang Dai-chien. This splash ink technique became a major force in her paintings. Kan, the disciple, became the designated successor to Chang Dai-chien. To widen her experience, Kan also studied for a time at the Ecole Des Beaux-Art, the Academic de La Grande Chaumiere in Paris, and the Art Students League in New York.

In her work, Kan fearlessly carries the Po Mo technique to new heights with the power of colors shaping her vision of nature. Her work has been shown in major museums around the world, and she is in collections ranging from the Metropolitan Museum of Art to the Taiwan Museum of Art, and in many private collections. She was the subject of an award winning film, "Eastern Spirit, Western World: Profile of Diana Kan," which premiered at the Boston Museum of Fine Arts and at the Smithsonian Institution in Washington, D.C. She has written a definitive book on Chinese painting titled *The How and Why of Chinese Painting*. And she has received numerous awards and citations including being the first Chinese woman painter in the United States to be elected as a National Academician.

Diana Kan is an elegantly tailored person of petite stature possessing immense energy and vision and is a lover of New York City where she lives and roots for the New York Mets baseball team.

DONG KINGMAN
(1911 – 2000)

Dong Kingman was born in Oakland, California. When he was five years old his family moved to Hong Kong. There he attended Lingnan School where he learned English and painting. His Paris trained art teacher was Szetu Wei, who "took me to outside painting. I learned to paint with him and that is many years gone by, but I learned to paint from him in the early days — about 1926."

In 1929, Kingman returned to Oakland where he and a friend bought a restaurant for $75. It was a bargain but their business was bad. "So in the afternoon I had time, so I went to art school to study painting. There was a place called Fox and Morgan, that's the school where I studied. I went there every Friday for outdoor sketching, for painting outdoors. I was using oil painting in those days, and my teacher after five or six lessons called me into the office and said, 'You don't know how to paint, don't come here anymore, you don't know anything about painting.' But I didn't give up. I'd learned watercolor in Hong Kong so next week I brought back a watercolor, and the same teacher told me, 'You got something there—watercolor'." Dong Kingman has worked in watercolors since 1931.

When the Oakland restaurant venture failed, Dong Kingman moved across the bay to San Francisco where he worked as a cook and houseboy for an insurance agent named William Drew. On Sunday mornings, Kingman would paint San Francisco. In the early 30s he joined the Chinatown Watercolor Club, a mostly social place little devoted to making art. In 1936, his big break came when he and another painter exhibited at the Art Center Gallery on Montgomery Street. The art critic for the San Francisco News, Junius Cravens, gave him a rave review which was followed by other favorable writeups. Soon he was receiving invitations to shows as well as the First Purchase Prize of the San Francisco Art Association.

He needed income to support his young family so he applied to the WPA (Works Projects Administration) Art Department where he was promptly employed. He shared a studio space at 15 Hotaling Place with Raymond Pucchinelli in the Montgomery Block near the Black Cat Café where "we hung around...just for the fun—some of us young painters in those days." The WPA salary was $80 a month. The studio on Hotaling Place developed into a colony of famous artists and writers including Beniamino Bufano, Raymond Pucchinelli, Matthew Barnes, John Steinbeck, William Saroyan and many others. It was during the Hotaling days that Dong Kingman met his first collector, a man named William Gerstle who bought several of his paintings. Another collector and patron was Albert Bender, an insurance executive who purchased many of Kingman's paintings not to own but to donate to major museums in the United States.

In 1942-43, Dong Kingman received two Guggenheim Fellowships, which enabled him to travel all over the United States to paint the country. He was invited to give many classes and lectures in places including Hunter College and Mills College. He was drafted into the Army Infantry in 1944 but was rescued from a foot soldier's fate by an admirer of his work, Eleanor Roosevelt, who got him transferred into the O.S.S. (Office of Strategic Services) Art Department. While he was in the Army, he had his first major exhibition at the M.H. de Young Memorial Museum in San Francisco.

That same year he was given his first one-man show at the Midtown Gallery in New York City and was hired by *Fortune Magazine* to illustrate a story on China. Dong Kingman was launched as a major artist and master of the watercolor medium with many exhibitions, lectures and commissions. Among his later commissions was the poster for the 1996 Olympics in Atlanta, Georgia. He has created many paintings for opening titles of such films as "55 Days At Peking," "The World of Susie Wong" and "Flower Drum Song." His friend, the late cinematographer James Wong Howe, made him the subject of a short film in 1954 entitled "The World of Dong Kingman." He also served from 1960 to 1980 as a judge for the Miss Universe competition.

Dong Kingman passed in May of 2000. His artwork for the motion pictures was donated to the Academy's Margaret Herrick Library at the Center for Motion Picture Study. And in the famous "Stage" Delicatessen on Seventh Avenue in New York there is a special spot called "Kingman's Corner" named in his honor.

— SPA and IPA interview with Dong Kingman in 1996

JAMES LEONG
(born 1929)

James Leong was born and raised in San Francisco Chinatown. His first artistic endeavor was a "mural" he painted as a 3 year old child on a wall in the family's home. Though he was punished for this act of creative energy, it did not discourage him from later pursuing art.

His first real encounter with art came when he was introduced by his father, who worked as a domestic, to a co-worker named Alan Cole. Cole was an Arizona painter and glass plate photographer of the 1939 World's Fair on Treasure Island. Leong began oil painting lessons with Cole for the next six years but his father had plans for him to go into the medical profession. He studied pre-medicine and was admitted to the University of California at Berkeley. Leong won the career tussle by being awarded a scholarship to the California College of Arts and Crafts in Oakland.

In art school, Leong was influenced by his mentors Karl Bauman, Andre Boratko, Spencer Mackey, Drs. Eugen Neuhaus and Helmut Hungerlan. He was also inspired by visiting artists Walt Kuhn and Yasuo Kuniyoshi. In 1951, his studies were interrupted by the draft which placed him in the Army Language School in Monterey, California as an illustrator. He finished his M.F.A. in art after his discharge in 1952 and went on to pursue an M.A. in Art Education from San Francisco State University in 1955.

During this period, Leong hung out with fellow artists like Nathan Oliveira and Clayton Pinkerton at the famous bohemian spots in San Francisco, the Iron Pot Restaurant and Vesuvios Bar. These were inexpensive places for writers and artists like Dong Kingman and Mark Tobey to gather and talk about art. They were in the heart of North Beach near the City Lights Bookstore. This was the action place.

Leong painted his first real mural as part of his M.F.A. thesis at the College of Arts and Crafts. It depicted the history of the Chinese in America, for a boy's home. He later executed a similar 17 foot long mural for the first federally funded public housing project, Ping Yuen, in San Francisco Chinatown. A third mural was painted at San Francisco State University.

This period was the height of the McCarthy era paranoia and his Ping Yuen mural aroused suspicion. According to Leong, the FBI, the Kuomintang, and the Chinese Communist Party, each suspected him of hiding messages in his mural. None were found but the experience dampened Leong's outlook and the controversy put the mural into storage for several decades.

He won a Fulbright Fellowship in 1956 and left for the Norwegian woods and fjords to study the work of Edvard Munch and bas relief painting. Then he was awarded a Guggenheim grant to work at the American Academy in Rome. It was here that his painting career took off. His work was purchased by people like Stanley Marcus, Igor Stravinsky and Vincent Price. He hung out with artist friends like Cy Twombly, Jack Zajac, Warrington Colescott and many others. Leong's stay in Rome lasted 31 years. He had many exhibitions in Europe and America and was collected by many museums. To help support his family, Leong worked teaching and as an extra in movies like "The Godfather III" and "The Last Emperor" and television commercials.

James Leong moved back to the United States in 1990 and settled in Seattle, Washington, a city that reminds him of Rome. His 17 foot Ping Yuen mural "One Hundred Years, History of the Chinese in America" will be installed in the new home of the Chinese Historical Society of America and Chinese American National Museum in 2001.

JAMES YEH-JAU LIU
(born 1910)

James Liu can be found most days in his studio on Main Street in Tiburon, California. His Han Syi Studio has been a fixture in this charming bay-side community for over 30 years.

Liu, who is called "Jimmy" by close friends and "Professor" by others, was born in Changsha, Hunan, China in 1910. His art studies began when he learned the fine art of calligraphy from his father, an artist of note. Liu went on to the National Academy of Fine Arts in Hangchow from which he graduated in 1935. There he studied both Chinese brush painting and Western style drawing from his French trained teachers. This ended when Japan attacked China in 1937 and Liu was drafted into the Chinese National Army where he served under Chiang Kai-shek. At the end of World War II, Liu was sent by Chiang Kai-shek with selected others on a world tour of the outside to learn about the West. They were the first permitted to "go outside."

In 1949, Liu left mainland China for Taiwan where he served as the Director of Communications and Transportation and taught classes at the Taiwan National Academy of Art. In 1962, Liu decided to move and settled permanently in the United States. Once here, he was invited to teach Chinese painting by his friend Professor Kai-yu Hsu, at San Francisco State University's

Humanities School. And in 1967 he founded his Han Syi Studio where he teaches painting as well as creates his own images.

Liu's images are a fusion of things remembered from China and the north San Francisco Bay locale in Tiburon. He can paint beautiful plum blossoms, landscapes, figures, flowers and birds and then paint the scene around him such as the Golden Gate Bridge from Tiburon or San Francisco's bay and hills. His paintings exhibit his dexterity and skill with the brush as colors are applied to define space and create images giving many people great pleasure.

Professor Liu, at 90 years old, still paints every morning at home before going down to his Han Syi Studio to frame his paintings and greet friends and people visiting from all over the world. He is a familiar, energetic and cheerful figure on Main Street, Tiburon, U.S.A.

GEORGE MIYASAKI
(born 1935)

George Miyasaki left his family home on the big island of Hawaii after graduating from high school in 1953. With his generation he felt the grass was surely greener on this side. "I was so happy …to get out of that place and come out here."

His high school teacher encouraged him to try the California College of Arts and Crafts in Oakland because he had gone there. Miyasaki originally had thought of attending the school at the Honolulu Academy but felt "that's not going anyplace." At the College of Arts and Crafts, Miyasaki studied with teachers like Carol Purdie, Ralph Borge and Louis Miljarak for the basic courses. He was like a sponge taking everything in. "I was so hungry…I came from nothing, you know, I didn't have any background at all… I didn't even know who Picasso was…. I think I was lucky because my mind was so open and unhampered. I didn't have any kind of prejudice or anything."

His first major was advertising design because "I never thought of anything like fine arts. I didn't even know such things existed…," but this changed when he was introduced to lithography and painting courses. He had begun the shift toward fine art. He took lithography and learned the printmaking processes from Leon Goldin and began experimenting on his own. He found painting and drawing on stone to his liking.

Miyasaki's second lithography teacher was Nathan Oliveira, whom he considers his most influential mentor. He was "the one I got closest to…he was like a big brother to me…you know, when you really need somebody." The painter Richard Diebenkorn was another big influence. "His work was really beautiful." Miyasaki credits both Oliveira and Diebenkorn with stressing the "importance of doing your own thing and not jumping on band wagons."

In 1957 Miyasaki was awarded a John Hay Whitney Opportunity Fellowship enabling him to continue as a graduate student. It was in this period that his work in lithography with its colors, vigorous surfaces and imagery gained wide attention resulting in numerous exhibitions and awards. Miyasaki was also equally successful as a painter. In 1958, Miyasaki became an Assistant Professor at the College of Arts and Crafts and also a lecturer at Stanford University and finally a Professor of Art at the University of California in Berkeley. He retired in 1994 after 30 years of teaching and now devotes his time to his art.

— IPA interview with George Miyasaki in 1998

© Irene Poon 1997

JOHSEL NAMKUNG
(born 1919)

Johsel Namkung in many ways is a Renaissance man. He was born in Korea in 1919 where his theologian father was teaching Greek and Hebrew in a seminary. Namkung's interest in the arts was sparked by his oldest brother's involvement in the visual and literary fields.

In 1936, Namkung went to study music at Tokyo Conservatory of Music though he originally wanted to be a painter. At the Conservatory, he studied music, theory, voice and languages. He became proficient in many languages including German, which played a vital role in his mastery of the German lieder or song.

The Namkungs moved to Shanghai in 1941. Japan had occupied Shanghai, but westerners were given some freedom of movement. There Namkung and his late wife Mineko were active in the music scene. They helped organize the Shanghai Philharmonic Orchestra. Namkung often sang German songs as a soloist with the orchestra. The Namkungs lived in a compound affiliated with his father's seminary. There Namkung was exposed to many westerners and their styles.

In 1947, Namkung was convinced by friends to leave Shanghai for the United States. He chose to settle in Seattle, Washington. There he received a scholarship along with a teaching assistantship at the University of Washington to study music. Because of his great command of languages, Namkung was hired to teach Japanese in the University's Far Eastern Department. It was here that Namkung met the artist George Tsutakawa who would become a longterm friend until his passing in 1998.

Namkung's ability with languages also resulted in a job with Northwest Orient Airlines. By the time Namkung finished his graduate studies in music the airline had established a base in Seattle. He was employed by Northwest as a translator and aide to visiting dignitaries from Asia. Namkung was allowed to travel with the airline and began capturing in photographs places he visited. His interest in photography was awakened again.

In 1956, Namkung left the airline job and concentrated on his photography. He became the apprentice to Chao-chen Yang, a noted Seattle photographer and master of color technique. After almost a year as an apprentice, Namkung went to work for a professional photographic laboratory. His own color as well as black and white photographs were beginning to gain recognition in local shows such as the Seattle Photographic Society's Annual exhibitions at the Seattle Art Museum.

Namkung's friendship with George Tsutakawa was a valued one. Tsutakawa gave Namkung confidence and the sharing of a mutual interest in the arts. Namkung was introduced to artists like Paul Horiuchi, Mark Tobey, Kenneth Callahan and Morris Graves. He left his job at the photographic laboratory and found work as a photographic illustrator for art books. By then Namkung had taken leave from the performance side of music to concentrate solely on his photography.

In 1966, Namkung had his first solo show at the University of Washington's Henry Gallery. This was in conjunction with the publication of *The Olympic Rain Forest*. Then his photography was acknowledged with subsequent exhibitions at Reed College, a retrospective in 1973 at the Henry Gallery and an exhibition at the Focus Gallery in San Francisco. His images were large in scale and comfortably shown next to paintings and art of other media.

Namkung's only other formal photographic training besides his apprenticeship with Chao-chen Yang was a week long workshop with Ansel Adams in Carmel, California. His work like that of Adams was large in scale visually and physically. They both saw their work as likened to musical compositions. Though Adams was an influence, Namkung much admired the work of Edward Weston, Imogen Cunningham, Eliot Porter and Minor White. And Namkung had his own vision.

Johsel Namkung is a tall soft-spoken man with a bass voice living quietly in Seattle. He still occasionally sings German lieder and often goes alone to capture the visual music of the natural world in his photographs.

ARTHUR OKAMURA
(born 1932)

"I think I've always been an artist. I recall actually having a one-boy show when I was in kindergarten. There was actually an opening on a weekend or something like that. I always drew and I always thought I would be an artist and I became an artist."

Arthur Okamura was born in Long Beach, California in 1932. His childhood was spent there and in Compton, California until 1942 and World War II. Then his family was sent to the Santa Anita Assembly Center and soon after that to the camp at Amache, Colorado.

In 1945, after Internment, Okamura lived in Chicago where he finished his public schooling. While he was in high school, his art teacher referred him to a Chicago friend who had a silkscreen poster studio. Okamura got a job there "at 60 cents an hour sweeping the floors in his poster shop, and I racked pictures and I watched. I ended up working there for twelve years and becoming the artist at the studio mainly by watching." Of course he took high school classes too, and night classes at the American Academy which specialized in commercial art.

Things changed for Okamura when he went to the Art Institute of Chicago. "I started to see, take art history and get a view of history and art together. The Art Institute itself is this great museum. I used to have lunch in front of the 'Grand Jatte' every-day. Of course that's not true since eating is prohibited in the galleries. Willem de Kooning won his first major prize about 1951 in the American show with the painting 'Excavation,' and I started to be interested in what American painters were doing after first thinking everything was happening in Europe." Okamura was influenced by the Impressionists and painters like Van Gogh and Gauguin before he discovered the American painters.

He lived in Chicago for twelve years. After graduating from art school, he was awarded an Edward L. Ryerson, Foreign Travel Fellowship and ended up on the island of Majorca. There he started to paint abstractly and at the same time began writing poetry. Okamura was influenced by other Americans who were there, like Robert Creeley the poet and the painter John Altoon. They were close friends until Altoon's death in the 60s. Okamura recalls "they just kind of opened a lot of doors to me about what's happening out there in painting, what's happening with poetry, music and art."

During this period, Okamura's paintings started to take the form of long verticals, like Sung Dynasty scrolls. He called them images "that I would paint and see where they seemed to be like other kinds of Asian art that I had seen—the clouds, the mountains, the states. These concepts and forms from that period of my work made me realize the racial unconciousness I felt or even kind of saw in my inner vision. Somehow they came forth... it's the kind of feeling that I like. I'm always surprised by it. I like it when I'm surprised. It's unexpected, it's not planned. It's magic."

In 1959, Okamura settled in Bolinas, California permanently except for a short period in Berkeley where he shared a studio with artist friends like Peter Voulkos, George Miyasaki, Don Potts and others. He recalls the studio as a gathering place where friends worked together and had Saturday night poker games. This same period, Okamura taught art at the California College of Arts and Crafts in Oakland where he retired after thirty one years. But Bolinas is where Okamura feels most comfortable. For him "Bolinas has been a part of my art and always has. The ocean, the tide pools. So I've been here all these years and I could just paint here forever. There are so many things. And I paint pictures I think are good to look at. I don't mean I'm not an iconoclast, you know. I don't want to upset myself, I'm not into that. I'm a picture maker."

— IPA interview with Arthur Okamura 1998

© Irene Poon 1996

MINÉ OKUBO
(born 1912)

Miné Okubo's childhood was spent in the warmth of her birth-place, Riverside, California. Miné's mother was an accomplished calligrapher and painter and her father was a gardener. As a young child, Miné wanted to become an artist like her mother.

Miné's early education was spent in the schools of Riverside. At Riverside Junior College she was the art editor of the campus yearbook. One of her teachers there advised her to study art away from home up at the University of California. Miné went away to school in Berkeley. There she studied with Professor Jack Haley, whose specialty was fresco painting. Miné became an accomplished fresco and mural painter. During her Berkeley years she supported herself and her art by tutoring, waitressing, housework, sewing, even working as a field hand. She earned a University of California Bachelor of Arts Degree in 1935, followed a year later by a Master of Arts Degree.

In 1938 Miné won the Bertha Taussig Traveling Scholarship from the University of California. She now had the opportunity of a lifetime to experience Europe. She spent 1938 and 1939 back-packing her way around Europe taking in all the colors, sights and sounds. When she returned to the United States, she found work with the Federal Arts Project demonstrating fresco paint-ing at the Golden Gate International Exposition on Treasure Island in San Francisco. While she was there, the painter Diego Rivera was painting his huge mural on the theme of Pan American Unity (now housed at City College of San Francisco). Though Miné never worked with Rivera, she was caught up in the aura of his gigantic personality and the force of his art. In 1940, Miné was given a one person show at the San Francisco Museum of Art and was awarded the anonymous donor prize. This exhibition led to the University of California Honor Society Art Show and the awarding of the Anne Bremer prize in painting followed by a second exhibition at the San Francisco Museum of Art. Miné was on her way to recognition as an artist when the Second World War broke out and her life was rearranged by the hysteria and events of the time.

Miné was separated from her family by the evacuation of all west coast Japanese and Japanese Americans into internment camps. Miné became person number 13660. She was interned at Topaz, Utah. After the shock of relocation had subsided, Miné began to record in drawings and paintings the events of Topaz camp life. She along with Chiura Obata and others formed the Topaz Art School. Miné found others in the camp who had experience with school publications, and together they put out a literary and art magazine called *Trek*.

In 1944, *Fortune Magazine* offered Miné a job upon seeing some of the illustrations she did for *Trek*. Miné Okubo left Topaz and moved to New York City to work for *Fortune* on a special issue dealing with Japan. She worked on providing images for many major periodicals and newspapers from 1944 to 1952. She published her internment drawings in a book she wrote called *Citizen 13660* in 1946. Miné went on exhibiting her paintings and returned to the University of California at Berkeley in 1950-52 as a lecturer in art.

Today, Miné Okubo still lives in the tiny apartment in New York City where she began pursuing her art independently after the war ended. She continues to find the way to express her visions of life.

TADASHI SATO
(born 1923)

Tadashi Sato often goes fishing for Mamo over the reef at Nakalele on the island of Maui where he was born in 1923. Here he finds not only fish he's caught by the thousands but "sketches" for paintings in the natural setting of the reef and its surround.

Sato did not begin serious training in art until 1946 after his discharge from the Army. During World War II, he served as a military cartographer in Australia, New Guinea and the Philippines due to his drawing skills. He enrolled in a summer class at the Honolulu Academy of Arts taught by Ralston Crawford, an artist associated with the Precisionist movement. Crawford was impressed with Sato's work and encouraged him with a scholarship to the Brooklyn Museum of Art School.

In 1948, Sato left the tranquility of Hawaii for the bustle of New York. He studied with Stuart Davis, a painter associated with the Synthetic Cubism movement, at the Brooklyn Museum Art School and the Pratt Institute. Both Ralston Crawford and Stuart Davis were important influences in the shaping of Sato's seeing. These two mentors working with flattened forms in space and using bold colors and hard edges shaped Sato's early work. To make ends meet and support his family while in art school, Sato worked in the service industry as a waiter, room service attendant and bartender.

His big break came when a struggling actor friend introduced his work to the late actor Charles Laughton, who became a patron and got him a contract with the Willard Gallery. Now

Sato's work was collected by luminaries like Laughton, Cornelia Otis Skinner, and Burgess Meredith and exhibited in major museums, among them New York's Guggenheim, the Whitney, and the Museum of Modern Art. Sato was also commissioned to create many murals and mosaics for places like the War Memorial Center in Wailuku, various hospitals, the Hawaiian State Capitol, and most recently the new Convention Center in Honolulu.

In 1960, Sato left the city of New York and settled back into the natural surround of his birthplace, Maui. After his return, Sato's work moved further away from the saturated colors and hard edged abstractions of his mentors toward his personal softer layers of flatten forms and muted colors. Now his imagery is focused intently on nature.

Tadashi Sato goes fishing not only for the Mamo fish but to catch in his mind's eye his favorite blues and greens of the water, the forms and luminous translucent light for creating his own floating world.

KAY SEKIMACHI
(born 1926)

Kay Sekimachi was born in San Francisco in 1926 and grew up in Berkeley, California. She began drawing at an early age and learned Japanese and the art of calligraphy in after school programs.

Life was disrupted by World War II. The Sekimachi family was detained at the Tanforan Racetrack Assembly Center. There Sekimachi met Chiura Obata, a professor at the University of California at Berkeley, who started an art school to give the detainees a creative outlet in their time of detention. From him Sekimachi learned Japanese brush painting and drawing. Eventually, she and her family were interned at Camp Topaz in Utah where she met the energetic Miné Okubo who taught art and documented camp life in her drawings. Her spirit and friendship under adversity was an inspiration to Sekimachi.

While at Topaz, Sekimachi learned the traditional Japanese craft of Origami. This art of folding and sculpting paper into forms would play an important part in the shaping of Sekimachi's later work. After her release from Topaz in 1944, Sekimachi and her family moved to Cincinnati, Ohio where she worked at the famous Rookwood Pottery studios as a glazer.

In 1945, the family settled back in Berkeley and Sekimachi enrolled in the California College of Arts and Crafts to study painting, design and silkscreen printing. It was here that she saw her first loom and decided she would become a weaver. This ambition was so strongly set that she purchased a loom and quit the College of Arts and Crafts in 1949. She attended tuition free classes at the Berkeley Adult School to learn the basics of weaving.

In the 1950s, Sekimachi attended an eye opening lecture by Trude Guermonprez at the Pond Farm, a community of artists in Guerneville, California not unlike the famous Black Mountain College. Guermonprez, one of the major figures in modern weaving, showed Sekimachi the endless possibilities of weaving various materials together to define space, texture, light, shapes and feeling.

Sekimachi went back to the California College of Arts and Crafts to study with Guermonprez in the summers of 1954 and 1955. She also studied with Jack Lenor Larsen, a major guru of the textile arts, in the summer of 1956 at the Haystack Mountain School of Crafts in Maine. She began her own teaching career as a substitute for Guermonprez at the California College of Arts and Crafts. In 1956, she became an instructor for the San Francisco Community College and the Berkeley Adult School. She was financially secure and her work was gaining acceptance and attention. She has exhibited with the Contemporary Hand Weavers of California at the M.H. de Young Memorial Museum in San Francisco and her work is in major collections such as the American Craft Museum in New York.

Today, Kay Sekimachi lives in Berkeley with her husband Bob Stocksdale, a noted premier wood worker, and she continues to explore and experiment with ways to weave, fold and shape materials into things of beauty.

GEORGE TSUTAKAWA
(1910 – 1998)

George Tsutakawa was named after George Washington by his parents when he was born on Washington's Birthday in 1910 in Seattle, Washington. He was one of nine children. The Tsutakawa family settled in 1905 in the Volunteer Park area of Seattle where George's father ran a successful import-export business. In 1917, George and a brother were sent to live with relatives in Japan where he learned the traditional arts of calligraphy, literature, tea ceremonies and flower arranging. In 1918, George came back to Seattle to help in the family business and to attend high school, then college. Back in America, George had to learn English again. He also learned French as he hoped to go to Paris and study art.

At the Broadway High School in Seattle, George was encouraged by his teachers to study art. He immersed himself in learning printmaking and sculpture. In the 30s he entered the University of Washington as an art major. His mentor was Dudley Pratt, who came to teach at the University via Yale, the Boston Museum and the Pennsylvania Academy. George became Pratt's apprentice, and learned the many processes and materials involved in the making of public sculpture. Two other sculptors who influenced George were Dudley Carter who made large wood carvings and Alexander Archipenko who taught at the University in 1935-36. Later George would discover the work of Constantin Brancusi as well as Northwest Coast Native American totem poles as a source of inspiration.

In 1937, George left the University and returned to the family business. He found little time to make sculpture, so he turned to painting. He became friends with artists like Morris Graves and Mark Tobey who were immersed in the arts and traditions of China and Japan, expressed in painting, calligraphy and Zen. The Tsutakawa family store became a gathering place for George's many Japanese artist friends like Kenjiro Nomura and Kamekichi Tokita as well as people like Graves and Tobey.

In 1941, Pearl Harbor changed everything. The family business was seized and the family was split and sent to internment camps in Minidoka, Idaho and Tule Lake, California. George was inducted into the U.S. Army in 1942. Since he was an artist, he became a portrait painter of officers and the painter of murals for the officer's club. He was transferred to Fort Snelling, Minnesota where he taught the Japanese language to officers. After his discharge from the U.S. Army, George returned to the University of Washington on the G.I. Bill as a graduate student in art and also as a teacher of Japanese in the Far East Department. He began teaching part time in the School of Architecture at the University after receiving his Master of Fine Arts in sculpture. Then he started collaborating with architects and designers, especially George Nakashima, and made furniture and sculpture, as well as going on with painting and ceramics.

In the 1950s, George began to exhibit his work locally as well as internationally. During this period his signature "obos" sculptures echoing Himalayan stone forms began to take shape. He was introduced by his friend the photographer Johsel Namkung to a book by the late Supreme Court Justice, William O. Douglas, describing his travels in the Himalayas. This book described the obos or rock piles made by travelers in the mountains to signify thanks for safe passage.

These obos became the foundation of George's work, and the Tsutakawa home became a mecca for artists and friends. It was an exciting time as Allan Watts was making the world aware of the power of Zen and John Cage was turning elemental sounds into music.

In 1958, George began building his monumental fountains for public spaces. These fountains were a large step from the character of the obos, and water was a living part of each design. His first commission was for the Seattle Public Library's plaza. In his lifetime, George built over 60 fountains all over the world.

George Tsutakawa devoted his life to art, and the tradition is carried on today by his four children who in their own right have made their imprints in art and music.

TSENG YUHO
(born 1925)

Tseng Yuho comes from a long line of illustrious ancestors. She claims seventy-three generations of Tseng Shen, the principal disciples and recorders of the Confucius sayings. She was born in Beijing in 1925. Her father was a naval officer, her mother a liberated Chinese woman who graduated from teacher's college and taught primary school. The family enjoyed the privileges of their social class, such as the Beijing Opera and tending their flowers and goldfish in their beautiful Chinese style house and courtyards, until the Japanese invasion.

As a child, Tseng Yuho was close to her grandmother who taught her embroidery and painting. From her mother she learned the importance of making a difference in society by not wasting one's time. At 11 years old, she was stricken with a near death experience in pleurisy. During her hospitalization, she painted portraits of movie stars like Shirley Temple and hung them around her bedside. Her doctor, impressed by her talent, told her parents she must study art. They agreed and Tseng Yuho began studying classical Chinese painting. Her father was a student in the informal painting salon of Prince Pu Jin, one of the three princes from whom the last Emperor was chosen by the Empress Dowager. Her father showed his daughter's paintings to the prince. She was invited to join their painting sessions. There she helped as a studio assistant learning to straighten paper and grind inks.

In 1939, Tseng Yuho was admitted to the Art Department of the Catholic Furen University. There she studied and painted classical Chinese landscapes, figures, flowers, birds, as well as the art of seal engraving. After graduation, she concentrated on the disciplines of the classical literatis. This included poetry, calligraphy and connoisseurship. She continued to study with Pu Jin, his brothers Pu Quan and Qi Gong, as well as taking courses on Chinese art history and aesthetics. She became an assistant to Pu Quan and later to the European art historian, Gustave Ecke, whom she married in 1945.

Tseng Yuho and Gustave Ecke left China in 1948. In 1949, Ecke was invited to Hawaii as Curator of Asian Art at the Honolulu Academy of Arts. Both she and Ecke worked at the museum and taught at the University of Hawaii. They also traveled wide and far giving lectures on art and art history. This same year, the noted art historian, Michael Sullivan, discovered her work and wrote about it in his book on contemporary Chinese art. He continues to have highest regard for her work.

In 1959, she was singled out for a one person exhibition at the Walker Art Center. She was the youngest artist represented by the prominent Downtown Gallery in New York. Some of her fellow artists in this gallery group were Stuart Davis, Charles Demuth, Ben Shahn, Max Weber, Yasuo Kuniyoshi and Georgia O'Keeffe. She also received great encouragement from the likes of Man Ray, who photographed her, Max Ernst and Andre Masson. Her work was recognized internationally. She has said of her work "All the historical knowledge and personal substantial experiences have matured my mind. I am thoroughly a contemporary artist, my art works have inspirations from old and new, both East and West, at the same time—neither East nor West."

Today, Tseng Yuho, called "Betty" by her friends, still lives in the Hawaii that she and her late husband came to in 1949. She has said "The first years from the cosmopolitan Beijing to the isolated Hawaii island, I did feel left out of the mainstream of intellectual life. However, kind friendships enchanted our daily life. The green hills and blue ocean remind us of the nobility of nature. After my war torn years in China and the years of Gustave Ecke in Germany, Hawaii is indeed a paradise."

IPA written interview with Tseng Yuho 1997

CARLOS VILLA
(born 1936)

Carlos Villa, an Asian American of Filipino descent, was born in San Francisco's Tenderloin District in 1936. He described himself in a 1992 conference on multiethnic identity at the San Francisco Art Institute as "…a Filipino not born in the Philippines—I am an American, not fully accepted because I am a Filipino in America."

He was one of two children in a family active in the Filipino community. His father worked as a janitor and was instrumental in organizing help for newcomers to the United States. Villa often accompanied his mother who worked as a maid. As she worked, young Villa occupied his time drawing. While he was growing up, Villa's boyhood hero was his cousin Leo Valledor who was a year younger and a budding artist.

Villa attended Catholic and public schools and hung out comfortably with other minority kids. His cousin Leo was already becoming an accomplished painter and Villa was becoming enamored of turpentine and oil paints. During the mid-1950s, Villa joined the army and was stationed in several states, spending his last two years in Korea as a clerk typist. In Korea he saw the film "Lust For Life," and was impressed with the story of Van Gogh.

In 1957, Villa returned home to San Francisco and took drawing lessons from Valledor. Through Valledor, he met many other artists, such as Jay de Feo, Wally Hedrick, Joan Brown and Manuel Neri. He soon enrolled at the California School of Fine Arts, now the San Francisco Art Institute.

In 1961, Villa graduated from the California School of Fine Arts with a B.F.A. This was a period of total art immersion for Villa. It was a small, friendly community of art students and faculty. The faculty included many luminaries of the Bay Area art scene, like Richard Diebenkorn, Elmer Bischoff, Frank Lobdell, Fred Martin and Manuel Neri. And Villa's fellow students included Joan Brown, Ron Davis, William T. Wiley and Robert Hudson. These people would become as famous as their teachers.

It was here that Villa was introduced to non-traditional media by Neri. This included working in plaster, wire and painting on plaster. In 1958, he was included in a group exhibition curated by Bruce Conner and a two person show with Joan Brown. Villa's work was noticed.

After graduating at the School of Fine Arts, he enrolled at Mills College. There he studied with Ralph du Casse and Peter Voulkos. Villa also absorbed art history when he became a teaching assistant to the art historian Alfred Neumeyer. At this time, Villa's work was included in several important exhibitions. Among them "Fifteen Bay Area Artists" at the Poindexter Gallery in New York and the Bolles Gallery, San Francisco, where his work was reviewed by Walter Hopps in "Artforum." He graduated from Mills in 1963 with an M.F.A.

The mid-1960s found Villa living in Los Angeles and then New York. His work was moving from painting to sculpture back to painting and mixed media. But became discontented with the New York Scene and moved back to San Francisco in 1969. Back home, he began what would be a lifelong involvement in multicultural activism and identity. He began teaching in an art program at the Telegraph Hill Neighborhood Center, and was hired to head the interdepartmental studies area at the San Francisco Art Institute. His artwork now incorporated feathers, mirror, bone, spit, sperm, cowrie shells, hair, silk, blood and other materials with paint and canvas. The work was widely exhibited. In 1973, Villa received an NEA grant and the Adaline Kent Award from the San Francisco Art Institute the following year.

Villa continues to receive many awards and inclusion in exhibitions throughout the country. He has taught at Sacramento State College and now at the San Francisco Art Institute. It is here that Villa envisioned a series of multicultural symposia involving many Bay Area and national speakers, among them Guillermo Gomez-Pena, Lucy R. Lippard, Moira Roth and Jaune Quick-to-See Smith. From this series was spawned his popular class "Worlds in Collision" and an art education program where art students work directly with inner city children.

Today, Carlos Villa is still actively involved in the multicultural landscape with his social concern, his art and his teaching.

C.C. WANG (WANG CHI-CH'IEN)
(born 1907)

"I call my paintings 'calligraphic images' because they express brushwork in its purest sense. I use all the different techniques found in Chinese painting, but leave out the 'story' or the narrative aspect of the painting. Concentrating mainly on brushwork is like listening to pure sounds in music. My main purpose is to sing with the brush." This statement was made by C.C. Wang in an exhibition catalogue for the art exhibition called "The Living Brush" in San Francisco.

C.C. Wang was born in 1907 in Soochow, China. He was taught painting early in life by Ku Lin-shih, one of China's prominent painters and collectors in Soochow. Wang later enrolled at the Soochow University in Shanghai to study law. He also continued his study of Chinese painting with the noted Wu Hu-fan. Wang received the best training in the mastery of the brush techniques of the masters and at the same time was introduced to connoisseurship.

In 1934–35, Wang was appointed an advisor to the Committee of the London Exhibition of Chinese Art. This was a wonderful opportunity for him since it gave him privileged access and opportunity to study the entire collection of the Palace Museum. From this unique experience, Wang would become the leading collector and connoisseur of Chinese art.

In the 1940s, Wang began teaching in the academies of art in Soochow and Shanghai. He also collaborated with the German art historian Victoria Contag on what is still regarded as the definitive reference for students of Chinese painting, *Seals of Chinese Painters and Collectors of the Ming and Ch'ing Periods*. During this time, Wang and his family made the big move to the United States settling in New York City. He had made earlier visits to tour collections of Chinese painting in American collections. Through the years, Wang has taught and lectured at American and Asian universities, and advised museums and collectors on Chinese painting.

In New York, Wang was exposed to modern art in the West. He was interested in the connection of traditional Chinese painting and the abstract art of the West. Artists like Mark Tobey, Franz Kline and Robert Motherwell in turn have been inspired in their work by Chinese Calligraphy, considered the foundation of painting in China. Now, having been introduced to abstract art, Wang joined the Art Students League in New York to immerse himself in Western painting techniques.

After his sojourn at the Art Students League, Wang's work took on a more spontaneous quality. His brushstrokes were looser and bolder. He started to apply ink in different ways as well as crinkling paper for compositional effect. This was the opposite of the studied way of traditional Chinese painting. His work fused the traditions of East with the innovative bravado spirit of the West. He had merged calligraphy and painting into his abstractions.

Wang's work has been exhibited in many places including the Asian Art Museum of San Francisco, Columbia University in New York, the Honolulu Academy of Arts and the Hugh Moss Gallery in London, England. The Metropolitan Museum of Art in New York was the fortunate recipient of some major Chinese paintings from Wang's extensive collection, Wang being regarded as the most respected connoisseur of Chinese painting.

C.C. Wang has been acknowledged for his mastery of the brush in translating his vision. He said in the catalogue for "The Living Brush" exhibition, "I often like to compare Chinese painting to Western opera. The brushwork in a painting is like the voice in an opera. That voice is pure music. I am trying to pay more attention to the abstract quality of the voice and less to the narrative part of the singing. Now I am doing paintings that pay even more attention to the brush-voice and the pure brush music. I try to sing and compose at the same time."

ANNA WU WEAKLAND
(born 1924)

Anna Wu Weakland was born in Shanghai, China in 1924. Her father was her first role model. He was a product of American Protestant Christian missionary upbringing. Wu proudly recounts how her father was one of the first two pupils at the University of Shanghai opened by Baptist missionaries. From there, the missionaries sent him to the United States where he studied and graduated from Columbia University, the University of Chicago and from the Rockefeller Theological Seminary in Rochester New York with a degree in theology. Her father returned to China with degrees and distinction and eventually became a Protestant minister, a lawyer, an educator and a publisher in Shanghai.

Wu followed in her father's footsteps and graduated from the University of Shanghai in 1943. She worked in an advertising agency. She was a liberated woman whose father insisted that all his children, girls included, become well educated.

In 1947, Anna left China for the United States. Emulating her father, she enrolled at Columbia University to study sociology. There she received a Master of Arts degree in 1948 and began working toward a Ph.D. But her course changed directions.

While in New York City, she often gave presentations at the China Institute to introduce Americans to China and its culture. Wu was proficient in both English and the different dialects of the Chinese language and was asked by the dean of the graduate school at Columbia to be the translator for a noted Chinese artist in New York to curate an exhibition at the Metropolitan Museum of Art.

The artist was Wang Ya-chun. Wu became his translator and it changed her life. "It opened the door for me, the whole world of Chinese art. This Professor Wang was one of the top artists from Shanghai, who brought the best contemporary Chinese art of that time to be shown at the Metropolitan Museum of Art, and I was to become his spokesman. So I saw all of his work and it opened my eyes and my heart just fell around to all these marvelous things...." Wu went on to his apartment for private lessons after her classes at Columbia. "He was my mentor,

absolutely." She later became his assistant when he couldn't return to China due to the communist takeover in 1949.

Professor Wang was famous for his rendering of goldfish. In the Chinese tradition, many painters specialized in certain subjects, like birds, chickens, flowers and landscapes. Wu studied the work and brush stroke techniques of masters like Ch'i Pai-shih who was considered the father of modern Chinese painting, and Chang Dai-chien, regarded as the master of masters.

Wu recalls that Chang Dai-chien "came to New York quite often while I was there so I took him shopping for his family and also had the chance to spend a lot of time with him, watching him paint." She also went with him to Hong Kong and later to Carmel, California. Wu liked "that period best, he's colorful, his colors were subtle and that was his really creative period...his later work was his real creative genius."

Besides studying Chinese art and painting, Wu also spent two years as a graduate student in Western painting at Stanford University. "I saw how the Western masters use their paints—I studied oil, watercolor and drawing." Wu and her late husband, a Stanford Professor, settled happily in California from New York. She said "the Bay Area gives you nature (and) fresh air. Nature encourages you to be creative, and I could work from 8 a.m. to 6:30 p.m. After long hours working, then sports." Wu is an avid tennis player and aerobic dancer.

Anna Wu Weakland continues to learn and to teach others in the schools and art programs at senior centers. She has been awarded many honors for her community work, including recently the Lifetime Achievement Award from the city of Palo Alto where she lives. She energetically pursues her painting, printmaking and designs for tapestries and ceramics. She believes "all the artists borrow ideas, it's how you borrow, how you use it. I borrow and use it, it enriches my work. Make it my own. My hopes are very wide, I like to continue to produce good work, continue my learning process, continue to do new things."

IPA interview with Anna Wu Weakland 1997

CHARLES WONG
(born 1922)

Charles Wong is an intensely private man of gentle demeanor and humor. He was born in 1922 within the "boundaries where, Broadway below Montgomery St., beyond Pine St., and Powell St." lies San Francisco Chinatown. "It was unwritten, but somehow, that was our boundary…the ghetto."

He took art classes in high school after which he received a scholarship to the California School of Fine Arts in 1939-1940. "I have this urge to do something in art…" This was interrupted by World War II, when Wong joined the Air Force. He returned to the California School of Fine Arts to study photography in the newly founded program of Ansel Adams. Wong thought "photography is something that I might be able to do more realistic. So I thought give photography a crack." There he studied with Adams, Edward Weston, Minor White and Imogen Cunningham.

Wong created photographs in series that had a "beginning, climax and an end…I'm not a one photograph person." He documented the Chinese community "because it was there, and I was one of them…. to photograph it was like getting it off my chest." A part of one of these series "Year of the Dragon" was featured in a 1952 issue of *Aperture*.

He was part of a group of "about 20 photographers. And we went around and photographed, and we did produce two large showings…one of them was the Discovery Show." Wong seems to recall this group showing at the San Francisco Museum of Art and the Eastman House around 1951-52. The group was loosely knit and lasted about "a year and a half or so…Then we got to the point of exhaustion. I think we just burned ourselves out. And then, it just dissipated. Everybody went home." Charles Wong's photographic career lasted only three years, or as he put it, "I just produced, I had to get it out of my system. And that's it. After that I went back to work and I forgot all about photography." He says now, "I have lived a good life, been a good person, that's all I want."

IPA interview with Charles Wong 1999

JADE SNOW WONG
(born 1922)

Jade Snow Wong, the fifth daughter in a family of six girls and three boys, was born on a wintry January day in San Francisco's Chinatown. The day was special and rare because it snowed—giving her her Chinese name.

Jade Snow was brought up in the strict discipline of a traditional Chinese family. She attended American public schools as well as a Chinese language school afterwards.

Jade Snow left the shelter of Chinatown to begin her junior high school years where she encountered her first taste of racism when she was taunted for being Chinese. She was undaunted and pursued her education.

While in school she worked at various housekeeping jobs which exposed her to the ways of American life. Jade Snow went on to higher education which was not usual for a Chinese girl at the time. She enrolled at San Francisco Junior College and eventually on to a university. The family she worked for to earn her way through college took an interest in Jade Snow's educational ambitions and suggested she meet the president of Mills College. Mills was then considered a small and "exclusive" women's college in Oakland. Jade Snow was hesitant because of the cost of tuition, but the president, Dr. Aurelia Reinhardt, was determined for Jade Snow to enter Mills. She found her work and a room in the dean's home on the campus.

Mills College changed the direction of Jade Snow's life. She graduated with honor and distinction in 1942 in her major of economics and sociology, and won membership in the Phi Beta Kappa honor society. After graduation, she was given the opportunity by a benefactor to take a summer course at Mills. Jade Snow chose to study pottery with Carlton Ball, the pre-eminent practitioner of studio pottery, and attended seminars in glaze calculation with Charles Merritt and lectures on pottery as art from Bernard Leach. World War II found Jade Snow

working as a secretary in a shipyard office where she submitted a winning essay on decreasing absenteeism in the workplace and won the honor of christening a new Liberty Ship.

At war's end, Jade Snow was invited to join the Ceramics Guild at Mills College. She produced a sizable body of ceramic ware and also learned from Carlton Ball the art of glazing on copper forms. Jade Snow decided she could earn a living selling her ceramics and rented a storefront on Grant Avenue in Chinatown to set up shop as a potter. The storefront pottery studio was a success in that the Chinese community thought she was crazy, creating a spectacle of herself, but the outside community bought her pottery as fast as she could produce them. About this time, Jade Snow discovered she was also becoming a writer. She had occasionally submitted stories to magazines such as *Holiday* and *Common Ground*. Her writing attracted the attention of the editor of Harper & Row who was interested in publishing "ethnic" stories. The editor gave her 5 years to write a book based on her experiences of growing up Chinese-American

Now Jade Snow had 2 careers—potter and enamelware artist, and writer. Her book *Fifth Chinese Daughter* was published in 1950 and her pottery and enamels began to be shown in museums such as the Art Institute in Chicago and the Museum of Modern Art in New York City. In 1958, Jade Snow and her husband opened a travel agency and shop to carry her work as well as gift items. In 1975, she published her second book, *No Chinese Stranger*. She no longer makes pottery but is still actively running her travel agency and gift store, and working on her third book.

Jade Snow Wong has said of her work, "My abiding motivation in both pottery and enamels is that…let's say it's a Sunday or any day…I spent that time at that place and that is a mirror of me at that time."

— IPA interview with Jade Snow Wong 1997

© Irene Poon 1996

To friends of several decades
George and Lucille Jewett
with admiration and affection
Jade Snow Wong, San Francisco
Christmas, 2001

© Irene Poon 1995

NANYING STELLA WONG
(born 1914)

"Moving from painting to prose to poetry to song to dance in my endeavor to express my longing for truth, beauty, compassion and peace and to understand from my life's experiences the meaning of our human existence, our kinship to other beings, globally and galactically"—the creed of Stella Wong.

Nanying Stella Wong was born in Oakland, California in 1914. She was educated in the public school system. While she was in grade school, Wong recalls how her teacher "would put her legs up on her desk, relax and make me go to each student in the class and show them how to draw. I don't know why. I just remember she made me do it. I remember even then my drawings. I remember the children would give me their heirlooms, you know. Their parents didn't know about it. Like a ring for my pictures. So that's how I began and then I got a lot of encouragement at Tech High" (Oakland Technical High School).

1932 was a memorable year for Wong. "I had motivation and Gladys Elam's influence was very strong. The more I think about it, I now believe my art and creative writing interest really began at Technical High School because of a certain art teacher, Gladys Elam. I just love to draw and to write, that was all I had to focus on."

Her teacher Gladys Elam believed in the strength of Wong's work and entered her art and literary works in the National Scholastic Art Exhibition. Wong won three third places, being the only one out of 7,000 finalists to achieve this. On the strength of these prizes and her work, Wong received a scholarship to the California College of Arts and Crafts in Oakland. She was already taking summer classes there while in high school.

At the College of Arts and Crafts, Wong learned watercolor painting from Ethel Adair. Wong's watercolor subjects were people and scenes from daily life. "I just simply painted what I saw before me." One of her watercolors from her San Francisco Chinatown series echoes her often published poem 'Angel Island.' "I chose painting 'Angel Island' with its stormy waves to set the mood of its tortured human history—this tale of the Chinese Plymouth Rock. Immigrants sometimes saw the beautiful view as their sailing ship was near San Francisco, but they were detained on Angel Island. Many never reached the city's shore."

Wong's painting and writing often worked in concert. Wong was simultaneously attending the University of California at Berkeley where she studied writing with Margaret Shedd. Wong graduated with a B.A. from the University of California in 1933 and from Arts and Crafts in 1935.

During this period, she met some Chinese American artists who lived in a building on the Montgomery Block in San Francisco. This area was a Bohemian community of artists and writers. These artists included Chee Chin S. Cheung Lee, Suey Wong and David Chun. Wong was invited to join and exhibit her paintings in the newly formed Chinese Art Association's exhibition at the M. H. de Young Memorial Museum in San Francisco. Later, she also became a member of the San Francisco Society of Women Artists.

In 1936, fresh out of Arts and Crafts, Wong painted a large 48" x 96" — masonite mural for Fong Fong, the first Bakery and Soda Fountain on Grant Avenue in San Francisco Chinatown. She did not receive payment for this. "All I got was the spray paint and the material to work on." She also designed the fountain's neon cornucopia ice cream cone as well as the tea sets and the menu covers.

The period of the late 1930s found Wong taking classes at Mills College in Oakland as well as at Cornell University at Ithaca New York. She studied and wrote poetry. While at Cornell, one of her wealthy classmates saw Wong's portfolio and got her a job designing jewelry for Helena Rubenstein. In 1939, Wong was invited by the Contemporary Masters Building Exhibition committee to show her work at the 1939 World's Fair on Treasure Island in San Francisco.

Around the early 1940s, Wong met the artists George Chann, Dong Kingman, and her late husband, the artist and photojournalist Kem Lee. Lee had a studio that became a gathering place for artists. Wong was the subject of an "impressionistic oil portrait" by Chann who had trained in Paris.

Wong's dual careers as an artist and poet have merged and divided in many exhibitions, competitions and publications through the years. She has made many friends in the literary world, especially Margaret Shedd and the American poet laureate William Carlos Williams, who in a letter to Wong said, "You know, one feels closer to some people than to others and I feel closer to you than some of my best friends or even relatives." Wong's poetry has won her many accolades as well as recognition in the International Who's Who In Poetry. And Wong carries these talents into her community work. She has received several California Arts Council Grants to present free art workshops to mostly senior citizens as well as children.

Nanying, who considers changing her middle name to "Starla," lives quietly in a modest house in Berkeley. She has said "I'm happy whenever I can express my deeper self—my words and pictures are at times in liaison with music, dance, light, with other painters, poets, dancers, musicians, then I'm even happier. Now I feel I've just begun to know what I'm searching for in art and literary expressions, and in life, but already I am a senior citizen, there is yet so much to learn."

— IPA Interview with Nanying Stella Wong 1997 and letters from Nanying "Starla" Wong to IPA

TYRUS WONG
(born 1910)

Tyrus Wong is an amazing man of high inventive energy. He has been a lithographer, calligrapher, muralist, painter, motion picture illustrator, greeting card designer and kite builder. Wong was born in Canton, China in 1910.

He came to the United States in 1920 with his father. He was left to live with other "bachelor" men while his father went to Los Angeles to seek work. Wong attended public schools but was easily bored and skipped school regularly. In junior high school, his art ability was evident as he made all the posters for his school's events. Though Wong was not academically inclined, the school's principal recognized his artistic talents and arranged a scholarship on which Wong to attended a summer session at the Otis Art Institute.

At Otis, Wong found his calling. He wanted to stay there to study art. His father was supportive and allowed him to drop out of junior high school. He managed to borrow money for Wong's first year tuition. The elder Wong did not want his son involved in sports, restaurant or laundry work. While at Otis, Wong worked part time in a Chinatown restaurant for meals and to help with expenses. There he met his late wife Ruth whom he married in 1937. After his first year, Wong received a five year scholarship. In 1935, his final year at Otis, he was awarded the Huntington Assistance Prize of $100 for being the top student.

Wong graduated from Otis as the Depression was gripping the country. He, like other artists, found employment with the Works Progress Administration. He was commissioned to make paintings and earned a salary of $94 a month.

In 1937, Wong was hired by the Disney Studios to do "in-betweening," flipping pictures to create the progressive action of movement of a cartoon character. He was bored with his job but his sketches attracted his supervisor who realized Wong was in the wrong department and transferred him to work on the classic feature film "Bambi." He was a pre-production illustrator responsible for creating the atmosphere, mood and keying the colors for each scene. What Wong did played a large role in the making of "Bambi" though he was not really acknowledged for it until recent years. Also, Wong was one of the first Asian Americans working in the motion picture industry and occasionally experience a taste of racism. "Bambi" was released in 1942. It was the beginning of Wong's long and illustrious association in the motion picture industry.

After four years at the Disney Studios, Wong spent the next twenty years working for Warner Brothers, RKO and Republic Studios. He made atmospheric sketches for such diverse films as "Harper," "The Wild Bunch," "Rebel Without a Cause," "Ice Palace," "The Sands of Iwo Jima," "The Fighting Kentuckian" and "Around the World in Eighty Days." Wong recalls that at Republic, he did a lot of John Wayne movies.

In the 1950s, Wong ventured into the greeting card world. He was the first Chinese artist to design greeting cards for major companies. Wong's designs were unique in that he blended seamlessly the soft atmospheric colors and brushwork of Chinese painting with traditional Christmas themes. His cards were bestsellers for twenty years for Hallmark, Looart, Metropolitan Greetings and Duncan McIntosh companies. In 1954 one design hit the one million mark in sales.

Aside from his work in the motion pictures and greeting card industries, Tyrus Wong was actively exhibiting his drawings, oil paintings, watercolors and lithographs. His work has been shown at the Library of Congress, Pennsylvania Academy of Fine Arts, Santa Barbara Museum of Art, Los Angeles County Museum, Brooklyn Museum and the San Francisco Museum of Art (now SF MOMA). Wong has won the Los Angeles Art Association Award, and the Los Angeles Museum Award for Watercolor in 1954, the Butler Institute of American Art Award, the 1960 American Watercolor Society's Kudner Prize as well as many other honors. His work is in the permanent collection of many museums as well as in private collections.

In the 60s, Wong became interested in kite making. He recalls seeing fantastic kites being flown as a child in China. He began by building simple one piece kites. Soon the pieces grew and the kites were made out of varied materials like rip-stop nylon, felt tip markers for coloring, rattan, fiberglass, marabou feathers or any natural of synthetic material. Now his kites are awesome constructions in their size, shapes and number of pieces. They can be comprised of as many as 25 butterflies or doves flying from a single line. Or a centipede of a hundred parts. His kites don't just fly in the wind, they are "free" to fly in different directions with life-like motion. They are alive and the many components interact as they fly. Wong has been acknowledged as a master kite maker by many kite magazines and organizations.

Tyrus Wong is a cheerful man of 90 years with twinkling eyes who still takes long walks near his home in Sunland, California. And fortunate is the person who sees him down on the Santa Monica pier flying his kites as they come to life in the southern California sky.

The following portfolio showcases the selected

works of 25 Asian American artists who have

made a great impact by paving the way for all

American artists by breaking down cultural,

social and economical barriers in the pursuit of

their art. Each of these visionary artists of the

older generation could easily be the subjects of

their own exhibitions and publications. This

selection is only a sampling of the diverse and

creative geniuses of this fine group of pioneers.

PORTFOLIO OF ARTISTS' WORK

⌘

Ruth Asawa
Woven Wire Sculpture, 1954
96 x 24 x 24"
woven metal
Collection of the Artist

Bernice Bing
Burney Falls, 1965
24 x 32"
watercolor
Estate of the Artist

Ruth Asawa
Untitled, mid 1970s
Bronze sculpture
10 x 18"
cast from wax-dipped woven wire
Collection of the Artist

Bernice Bing
Reclining Figure, 1962
60 x 60"
oil on canvas
Estate of the Artist

Mask in use in the Ballet
Performance from
the Movie "The King and I"
Photo by Yul Brynner

Wah Ming Chang
King and I Mask, 1956
16 x 13 1/2 x 10"
moulded rubber/ hand painted
surface and applied decoration
Collection of the Artist

Wah Ming Chang
Communicator,
from the "Star Trek" series
4 1/2 x 2 1/8
Moulded plastic and
hand wrought metal
Collection of the Artist

Benjamen Chinn
Untitled (mailboxes),
Washington Street below
Stockton (Chinatown),
San Francisco, 1947
9 1/2 x 7 1/2"
gelatin silver print
Collection of the Artist

Benjamen Chinn
Untitled, Chinatown, SF, 1947
4 1/2 x 3 3/4"
Gelatin silver print
Collection of the Artist

Taneyuki Dan Harada
Barracks: Topaz, Utah - 1944
22 x 28"
oil on canvas
Fine Art Museums of San Francisco, Museum
Purchase, Mildred Landstrom Trust, 1996.117

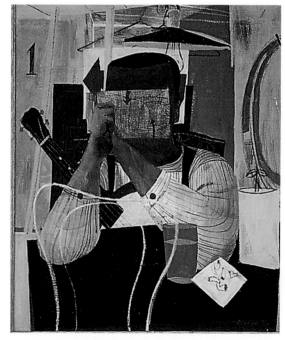

Taneyuki Dan Harada
Self Portrait, 1954
20 x 24"
oil on canvas
Collection of the Artist

Dale Joe
Ellipse-Eclipse, 1997
40 x 26"
oil, acrylic and ink on masonite
Collection of the Artist

Diana Kan
Dare to Dream, 1992
24 x 48"
Mineral, water color on gold leaf on silk
Collection of the Artist
Photo by Sing-Si Schwartz

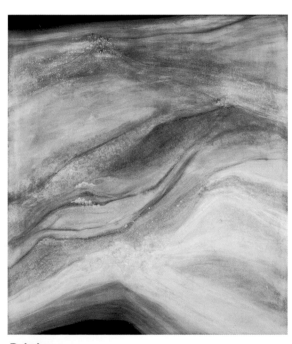

Dale Joe
Sungscape, 1957
60 x 52"
oil, acrylic on canvas
Collection of the Artist

Diana Kan
Day Break, 1995
23 1/4 x 17 1/4"
Mineral, water color on gold leaf on silk
Collection of the Artist
Photo by Sing-Si Schwartz

Dong Kingman
Four Horse Square, c. 1976
29 1/4 x 37 1/4"
watercolor on paper
Collection of Mr. and Mrs. Dong
Kingman, Jr.

Dong Kingman
Country Road, c. 1976
13 x 13 1/2"
watercolor on paper
Collection of Mr. and Mrs.
Dong Kingman, Jr.

James Leong
Vashon/Soochow, 2000
45 x 45"
mixed media
Collection of the Artist

James Leong
Erosions of a Timeless
Face, 1959
45 x 57 1/2"
mixed media
Collection of the Artist

James Yeh-jau Liu
Landscape, 2000
30 x 36"
ink and colors on paper
Collection of the Artist

James Yeh-jau Liu
Black and White Plum
Blossom, 2000
ink on paper
31 x 32"
Collection of the Artist

George Miyasaki
Rough Cut, 1999
72 x 90"
acrylic and construction on canvas
Collection of the Artist

George Miyasaki
Untitled #1, McAuley Series, 1958
40 1/2 x 40 1/2"
oil on canvas
Collection of the Artist

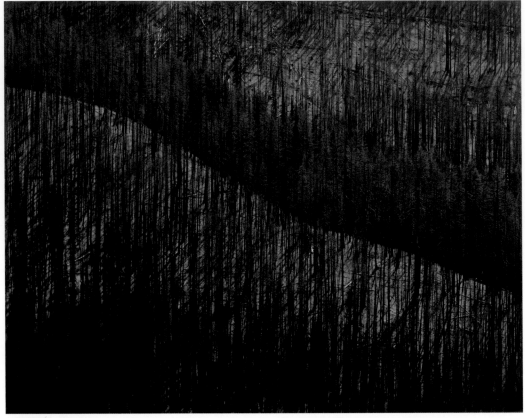

Johsel Namkung
Sherman Pass, 8/13/93
28 x 32"
ektacolor print
Collection of the Artist

Johsel Namkung
Shi Shi Beach, Olympic National Park, 6/21/80
28 x 32"
ektacolor print
Collection of the Artist

Johsel Namkung
Brewster Flat, 1/25/85
48 x 60"
ektacolor print
Collection of the Artist

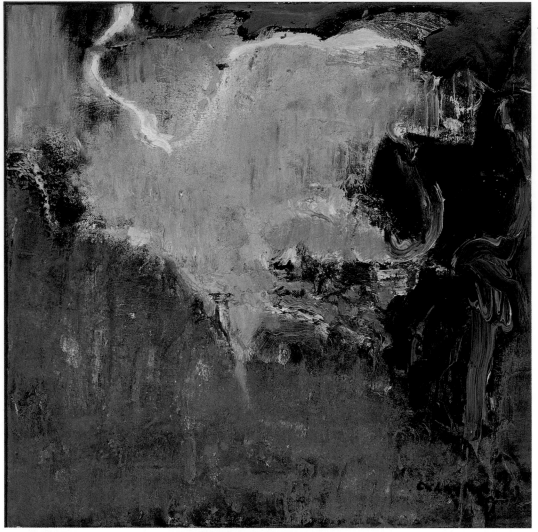

Arthur Okamura
Tide Pool, 1960
15 3/4 x 15 3/4"
oil on canvas
Collection of George Miyasaki

Arthur Okamura
Grouper, 1997
21 x 10 1/2 x 2"
acrylic/mixed paper media
Collection of Irene Poon and Stan Andersen

Mine Okubo
Orange Flowers, 1961
38 x 52"
oil on canvas
Collection of Drs. Hall
and Leeper

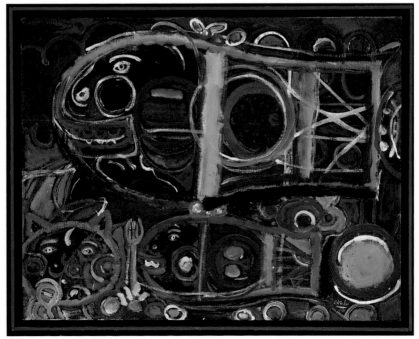

Mine Okubo
Fish, Fish, Cat — 1967
24 x 30 1/4"
acrylic on canvas
Collection of Drs. Hall and Leeper

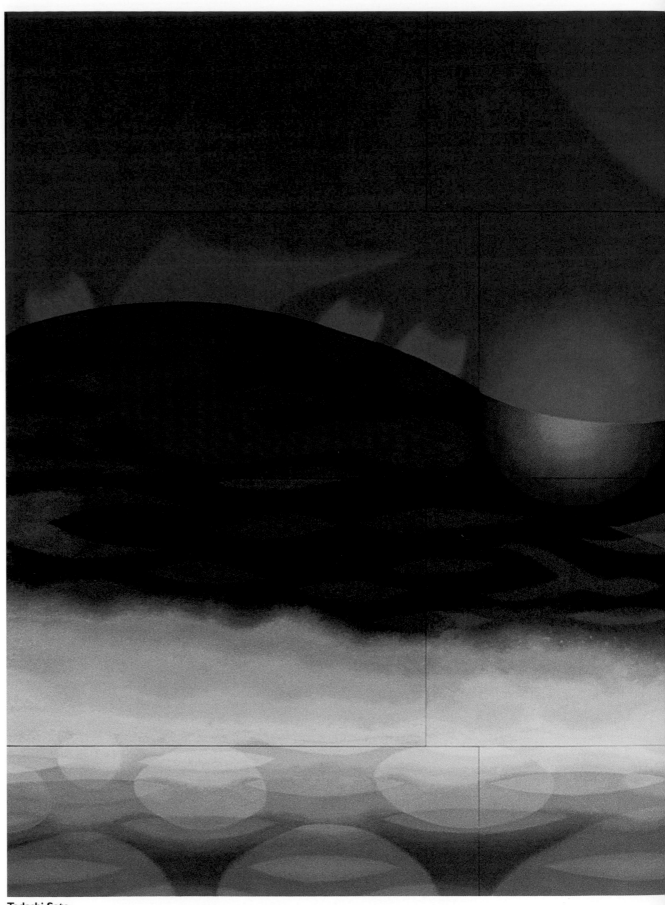

Tadashi Sato
Nakalele, 1997
17 x 26'
oil on linen
Hawaii State Foundation on Culture and the Arts
Photo by Douglas Peebles

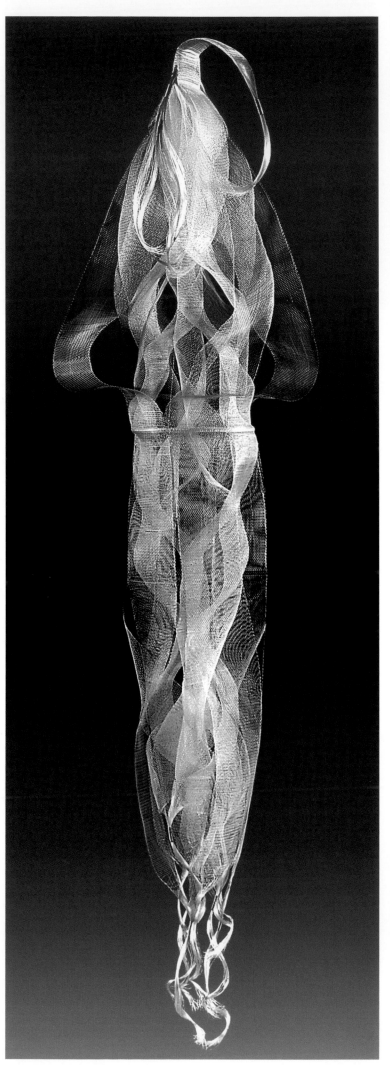

Kay Sekimachi
Amiyose V, 1994
85 x 13 x 9"
nylon monofilament
Collection of the Artist

Kay Sekimachi
Takarabako V, 1999
9 x 7 x 7"
linen
Collection of Forrest L. Merrill

George Tsutakawa
in his studio with maquettes
of fountains and sculptures,
circa 1980
Photo by Paul Macapia
Collection of the Tsutakawa
Family

George Tsutakawa
Song of the Forest, 1981
20'
bronze
Tsutsujigaoka Park, Sendai, Japan
Photo by Osamu Murai

Tseng Yuho
Midnight Chime, 1995
30 x 30"
acrylic and aluminum on paper
Private collection
(cover image)

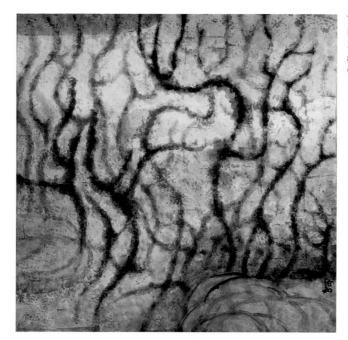

Tseng Yuho
Morning Walk, 1999
30 x 30"
acrylic and aluminum on paper
Collection of the Artist

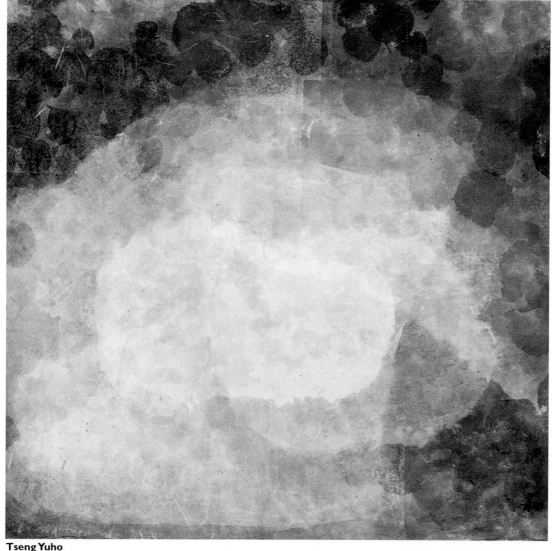

Tseng Yuho
Embrace Within, 1995
24 x 24"
acrylic on paper
Collection of the Artist

84

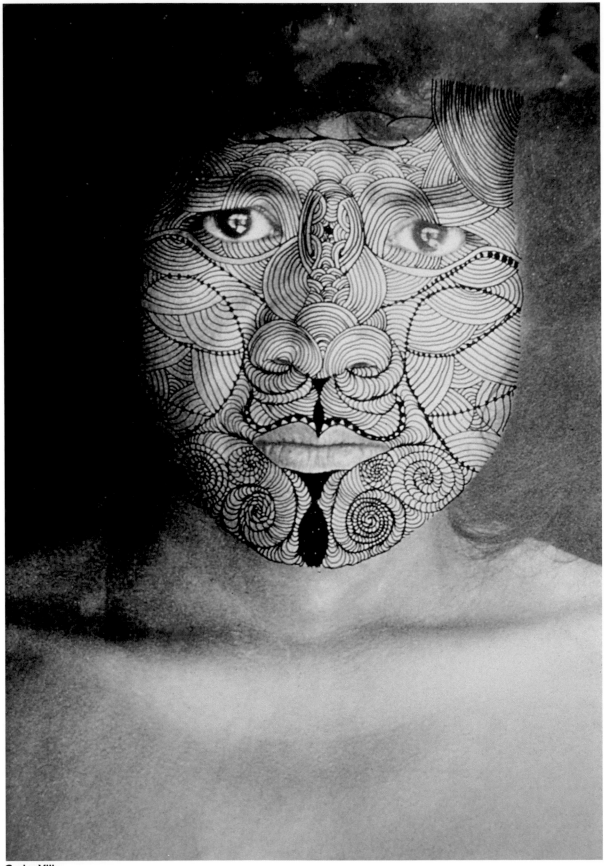

Carlos Villa
Tatu, 1969
22 x 18"
ink on itec print
Collection of the Artist

C.C. Wang
Landscape, 1961
22 1/8 x 15 3/4"
ink and color on paper
Collection of the
Phoenix Art Museum

Carlos Villa
Mom, 1978
39 x 25"
bone, hair, rags, comb, photograph
and acrylic on canvas
Collection of Sydney Matisse Villa

Anna Wu Weakland
Memories, 1993
82 x 42"
tapestry
Private collection

C.C. Wang
Calligraphic Abstraction
after Seal Script, 1998
54 1/4 x 27 1/2"
ink on paper
Private collection

Anna Wu Weakland
Cloud over the Mountain, 1989
22 x 30"
monotype
Collection of the Artist

Charles Wong
Year of the Dragon, 1952
11 x 14"
gelatin silver print
Collection of Irene Poon and Stan
Andersen

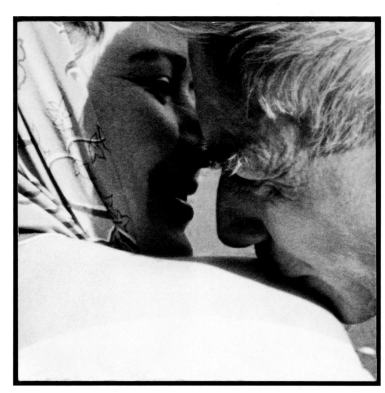

Charles Wong
The Lovers, 1956
9 3/4 x 12 3/4"
gelatin silver print
Collection of the Artist

Charles Wong
The Lovers, 1956
9 3/4 x 12 3/4"
gelatin silver print
Collection of the Artist

Jade Snow Wong
Bowls, 1995
H 4 1/2; Diam 10 3/4"
H 2; Diam 6"
H 2; Diam 4"
enamel on metal
Collection of Irene Poon and Stan Andersen

Nanying Stella Wong
Hang Ah Tearoom, c. 1940s
27 3/4 x 25"
watercolor on paper
Collection of the Artist

Jade Snow Wong
Large Bowl, 1946
Diam: 20"
ceramic
Collection of the Artist

Small Vase, 1942
H 6 1/4; Diam 3 3/4"
ceramic
Collection of Irene Poon and
Stan Andersen

Nanying Stella Wong
Angel Island, c. 1940s
17 1/2 x 27 5/8"
watercolor on paper
Collection of the Artist

Nanying Stella Wong
Flare, c. 1940s
22 1/2 x 30 5/8"
watercolor on paper
Collection of the Artist

Tyrus Wong
Old Barn
30 x 16"
Pastel
Collection of the Artist

Tyrus Wong
Newsboy
30 x 20"
ink on paper
Collection of the Artist

SELECTED BIBLIOGRAPHY

AWARDS • HONORS • EXHIBITIONS • FILMS • PUBLIC COLLECTIONS

RUTH ASAWA

Readings:

Ruth Asawa, A Retrospective View. San Francisco Museum of Art, 1973
Cookies and Bread: The Baker's Art. Museum of Contemporary Crafts New York, 1965
American Women: 20th Century. Lakeview Center for the Arts and Sciences, Peoria, Ill., 1972
50 West Coast Artists. Henry Hopkins and Mimi Jacobs. 1982
View From Asian California 1920-1965. Michael D. Brown. 1992
With New Eyes: Toward an Asian American Art History in the West. San Francisco State University,1995
"Japanese American Internment Memorial." *San Jose Mercury News,* March 5, 1994
The New Older Woman. Downes, Tuttle, Faul & Mudd. Celestial Arts, Berkeley, 1996

Awards:

American Institute of Architects, Fine Arts Gold Medal, 1974
Asian Heritage Council, Arts Award, 1989
Women's Caucus for Art, Outstanding Achievement in the Visual Arts, 1993
San Francisco Education Fund, Golden Apple Lifetime Achievement Award, 1995
San Francisco Art Institute, Honorary Doctorate of Fine Arts, 1997
San Francisco State University, Honorary Doctorate, 1998

Exhibitions:
Solo:
Design Research, Cambridge, Massachusetts, 1946
Peridot Gallery, New York, 1954 and 1956
M.H. de Young Memorial Museum, San Francisco, 1960
Pasadena Museum of Art, 1965
San Francisco City College Art Gallery, 1987

Group:
Sao Paulo Bienal, Brazil, 1955
The Whitney Sculpture Annual, Whitney Museum, New York, 1956
Los Angeles Museum of Contemporary Art, 1989-90
"With New Eyes: Toward an Asian American Art History in the West," Art Department Gallery, San Francisco State University, 1995
J.J. Brookings Gallery, San Francisco, 1995-1997

Collections:
Solomon Guggenheim Museum, New York City
Oakland Museum of California Art
Chase Manhattan Bank, New York City
Whitney Museum of American Art, New York City

BERNICE BING

Readings:

Rolling Renaissance, San Francisco Underground Art, 1945-1968.
Intersection and Glide Memorial Foundation, 1968
Artforum, Vol. 1, No. 2, 1964
Art in the San Francisco Bay Area.
Thomas Albright, University of California Press, 1985
With New Eyes: Toward an Asian American Art History in the West.
San Francisco State University, 1995
Bernice Bing. Moira Roth and Diane Tani, Visibility Press, 1991
Asian Traditions/Modern Expressions. Abrams/Rutgers University, 1997

Awards:

California College of Arts And Crafts Full Scholarship, 1956
San Francisco Art Institute Alumni Award, 1982
San Francisco Art Commission for Services to Community Arts, 1984
Asian Heritage Council Art Award, 1990
Women's Caucus for Art Honor Award, 1996

Exhibitions:
Solo
Batman Gallery, San Francisco, 1961
California College of Arts and Crafts, 1968
South of Market Cultural Center, San Francisco, 1991

Group
San Francisco Art Association 80th Annual Exhibition, San Francisco Museum of Art, 1960
Berkeley Art Gallery, 1963
Cellini Gallery, "Rolling Renaissance," San Francisco, 1968
San Francisco Art Institute Alumnae Exhibition, South of Market Cultural Center, San Francisco, 1983
"Chinese American Artists," Southern Exposure Gallery, San Francisco, 1990
"Three Artists," Asian American Arts Center, New York, 1993
"With New Eyes: Toward an Asian American Art History in the West," Art Department Gallery, San Francisco State University, 1995
"Asian Traditions/ Modern Expressions," Rutgers University, (traveling), 1997-1999

WAH MING CHANG

Readings:

Who's Who in California 1981-1982
Wah Ming Chang: Artist and Master of Special Effects. Gail Blasser Riley, 1995
The Life and Sculpture of Wah Ming Chang. David Barrow and Glen Chang, 1989
Star Trek: "Where No One Has Gone Before:" A History in Pictures.
Simon & Schuster, 1994
Disney's Art of Animation: From Mickey Mouse to Beauty and the Beast.
New York, Hyperion, 1991
Views From Asian California 1920-1965. Michael D. Brown, 1992

Awards:

Honolulu Academy of Arts, First Prize, 1938
Monterey County Fair, First Prize, 1977
Academy Award, Special Effects, "The Time Machine," 1960
International Motion Picture's CINE Golden Globe Award, "Ecology – Wanted Alive," 1973

Exhibitions:
Solo
City of Paris Department Store Gallery, San Francisco, 1925
Carmel Art Association, Carmel, California, 1981, 1989, 1993
Lawrence Gallery, Oregon, 1997
Monterey Museum of Art, Monterey, California, 2000

Group
East West Gallery, San Francisco, 1928
Brooklyn Society of Etchers, Brooklyn, New York, 1928
Honolulu Academy of Arts, 1928
Carmel Art Association, Carmel, California, 1983, 1987

Films:
Fantasia. Walt Disney, 1940
Bambi. Walt Disney, 1942
Pinocchio. Walt Disney, 1942
The King and I. Fox, 1956
Spartacus. MCA/Universal, 1960
The Time Machine. MGM/UA, 1960

Television Series/Special Effects:
The Outer Limits. 1963-1965
Star Trek. 1966-1970s

BENJAMEN CHINN

Readings:

Aperture No. 2. 1952
An American Century of Photography, Vol. II. Hallmark Cards, Inc., 1999

Awards/Honors:

Selected to West Coast Screening Committee, "Family of Man Exhibition," 1951

Exhibitions:
Solo
De Anza College Gallery, California, 1965

Group
"Perception," California Palace of the Legion of Honor, San Francisco, 1954
San Francisco Annual Arts Festival, San Francisco, 1960s (four consecutive years)
Mt. Angel College, Mt. Angel, Oregon, 1964
California School of Fine Arts 125th Anniversary Exhibit,
Focus Gallery, San Francisco, 1972
In Celebration of 50th Anniversary of Ansel Adams First Formal Photography
Class at the California School of Fine Arts,
Transamerica Gallery, San Francisco, 1998

Collections:

Hallmark Cards, Inc.

TANEYUKI DAN HARADA

Readings:

Views From Asian California 1920-1965. Michael D. Brown, 1992
The View From Within: Japanese American Art From The Internment Camps
1942-1945. Karin M. Higa/ Japanese American National Museum, 1992, 1994
With New Eyes: Toward an Asian American Art History in the West. San
Francisco State University, 1995
Asian Traditions/Modern Expressions. Abrams/ Rutgers University, 1997
Art of California Magazine, Sept. 1992
"A" Magazine (Inside Asian America), 1994
Fine Arts, Winter-Spring, Fine Arts Museum of San Francisco, 1998

Exhibitions:
Solo
Block 5, Tule Lake Segregation Center, California, 1945
KPFA-FM, Berkeley, 1950s
Grey Shed Gallery, Oakland, California, 1950s

Group
Oakland Art Gallery, 1948-49
San Francisco Museum of Art, 1948-49
California Palace of the Legion of Honor, San Francisco, 1948
"The View From Within" UCLA Wight Art Gallery, 1992 (traveled)
"With New Eyes: Toward an Asian American Art History in the West," Art
Department Gallery, San Francisco State University, 1995
"Asian Traditions/Modern Expressions," Rutgers University (traveling), 1997-1999
"Art After Incarceration," Pro Arts, Oakland, California, 1998

Collections:

Fine Arts Museums of San Francisco,
M.H. de Young Memorial Museum

DALE JOE

Readings:

Asian Traditions/Modern Expressions, Abrams/Rutgers University, 1997
Dale Joe: Paintings, Catalogue, The University of Iowa Museum of Art, 1999

Awards:

John Hay Whitney Fellowship Award, 1953-1954 to study in New York
Fulbright Award, 1956-1957 to study in France

Exhibitions:
Solo
Urban Gallery, New York City, 1954
Mi Chou Gallery, New York City, 1962-1963
The University of Iowa Museum of Art, 1999

Group
San Francisco Art Association Annual Exhibition, San Francisco Museum of Art,
1951, 1952, 1953
Bokujin (Ink-Men), Japan, 1954, 1955
Peintres Americains Fulbright, Paris, 1957
Fulbright Painters, Smithsonian (traveling exhibition), 1958
"Young America," Whitney Museum, New York City, 1960
"Asian Traditions/ Modern Expressions." Rutgers University, (traveling) 1997-
1999

Collections:

San Francisco Museum of Modern Art
Newark Museum of Art
New York University

DIANA KAN

Readings:

Harvard Asia Pacific Review, Winter, 1997-98
Asian Art News, March/ April 1996
Who's Who in American Art, 1969
The How And Why of Chinese Painting. Von Nostrand Reinhold, New York,
1974, Simon & Schuster, 1986
American Artist, November 1974
Who's Who in the World, 1984
Asian Abstractions/Modern Expressions. Abrams/Rutgers University, 1997

Awards/ Honors:

Accepted as pupil and disciple of Chang Dai-chien, 1946
Grumbacher Award, National Arts Club, New York, 1972
"Honored Artist of the Year," Catherine Lorillard Wolfe Art Club, 1983
Diana Kan Appreciation Day, June 1, 1991, Boston
National Academician, National Academy of Design, New York, 1994
Wayne Birschbach Award, National Academy of Design, New York, 1994

Exhibitions:
Solo
National Academy of Fine Arts, Shanghai, China, 1935
Gloucester Art Galleries, Hong Kong, 1946-1947
Jean Turner Art Galleries, San Francisco, 1950
El Monsout Art Galleries, Casablanca, 1952
National Historical Museum, Taiwan, 1971
National Arts Club, New York, 1979
Dyansen Gallery, New Orleans, Louisiana, 1989
L.J. Wenders Fine Arts Gallery, New York, 1993
Midtown Payson Galleries, Hobe Sound, Florida, 1996
National Museum of History, Taiwan, 1997

continued next page

Diana Kan continued

Group

Royal Academy of Fine Arts, London, 1963, 1964
"Four Artists" New Britain Museum, Connecticut, 1979
Invitational Exhibition, Museo De la Acuarela Mexiciania, Mexico City, 1989
"Asian Traditions/Modern Expressions," Rutgers University (traveling) 1997-1999

Collections:

Saint John's University, Shanghai, China
National Museum of History, Taiwan
Metropolitan Museum of Art, New York
Philadelphia Museum of Art
Nelson-Atkins Museum, Kansas City
Pensacola Museum of Art, Pensacola, Florida
National Academy of Design, New York
Government House, Vancouver, B.C.
Anchorage Museum of History and Art, Alaska

Films:

Eastern Spirit, Western World – Profile of Diana Kan, 1998 and 2000

DONG KINGMAN

Readings:

"A Report to the State Department' (drawings and text). Dong Kingman, *Life Magazine*, February 14, 1955
The Watercolors of Dong Kingman, and How The Artist Works.
Saroyan & Grushkin, New York Studio Publications, 1958
Artists and People. Yvonne Greer Thiel, Philosophical Library Inc., 1959
San Francisco: City On Golden Hills. Herb Caen & Dong Kingman.
Doubleday & Co., 1967
Dong Kingman's Watercolors. Dong Kingman & Helena Kuo Kingman.
Watson-Guptill Publications, 1980
Paint The Yellow Tiger, Dong Kingman. Sterling Publications, New York, 1991
Views From Asian California 1920-1965. Michael D. Brown, 1992
With New Eyes: Toward an Asian American Art History in the West.
San Francisco State University, 1995
Dong Kingman: Portraits of Cities. 22 Century Film Corp., New York, 1997

Awards:

First Purchase Prize, San Francisco Art Association, 1936
John Simon Guggenheim Foundation Grant, 1942, 1943

Exhibitions:
Solo
The Art Center, San Francisco, 1936
M.H. de Young Memorial Museum, San Francisco, 1945
Midtown Gallery, New York, 1945
Taipei Museum, 1996
Harmon-Meek Gallery, Naples, Florida, 1997
Brewster Gallery, New York, 1997
Academy of Art College, San Francisco, 1997
Chinese Historical Society of America, San Francisco, 2001 (posthumous)

Group
San Francisco Art Association, 1936
"With New Eyes: Toward an Asian American Art History in the West," Art Department Gallery, San Francisco State University, 1995
Rotary Club, City Hall, Hong Kong, 1997
Taipei Art Gallery, New York City, 1997

Film Titles:
World of Susie Wong. 1960
Flower Drum Song. 1961
55 Days at Peking. 1963
Circus World. 1964
King Rat. 1965
The Sand Pebbles. 1966
The Desperados. 1969
Lost Horizon. 1973
The World of Dong Kingman. James Wong Howe, 1954

Collections:
M.H. de Young Memorial Museum, San Francisco
Art Institute of Chicago
San Francisco Museum of Art
Hirschhorn Museum, Washington, D.C.
Metropolitan Museum Of Art, New York
Whitney Museum of Art, New York
Pennsylvania Academy of Fine Arts, Philadelphia
Margaret Herrick Library, Center for Motion Picture Study,
Motion Picture Academy, Los Angeles

JAMES LEONG

Readings:

Who's Who in the World. Marquis 4th, 5th Editions
Who's Who in American Art.
Dictionary of Contemporary Artists. Paul Cummings, Editor
Asian Art News, November-December 1994
"Northwest Asian Weekly," January 11-17, 1997 and April 1-7, 2000
"The News Tribune," August 24, 1997
Asian Traditions/Modern Expressions. Abrams/ Rutgers University, 1997

Awards:

John Hay Whitney Opportunity Fellowship to study in New York, 1953-56
Fulbright Grant to study in Norway, 1956-1959
John Simon Guggenheim Foundation Grant to study in Rome, 1959-1964

Exhibitions:
Solo
Barone Gallery, New York, 1955, 1956, 1957
American Gallery, Los Angeles, 1955
Haghfelt Gallery, Copenhagen, Denmark, 1957
Tyler School of Art in Rome, Temple University, Rome, 1967
Larcada Gallery, New York, 1975
Galleri Johan D. Galtung, Oslo, Norway, 1975
Studio Due, Rome, Italy, 1976
Lasater Gallery, Seattle, Washington, 1994

Group
Whitney Museum Annual, New York, 1956
Mi Chou Gallery, New York, 1958
Traveling Exhibition of Western Museums, 1956-1958
Gimpel Fils, Ltd., London, 1959
Palazzo Venezia, Rome, 1959
American Academy Annual, Rome, 1959
Casa Menotti, Spoleto, Italy, 1959
Galleria l'88, Rome, Italy, 1963
Gallery Daché, New York, 1966
Adele Bednarz Gallery, Los Angeles, 1966
"Asian Traditions/Modern Expressions," Rutgers University, (traveling) 1997-1999

Film/ Television:

Godfather III. Paramount, 1958
Mortacci. Unione International
Il Piccolo Diavolo. Yarno Productions
The Last Emperor. 1987
Animated Prologue Sequence/Titles, John Huston's *Freud, A Secret Passion*

Collections:

The Princeton Museum
New York University Museum
Rochester Museum
Harvard University
Dallas Museum of Fine Arts
Indianapolis Museum of Art
The Georgia Museum
The Weatherspoon Art Gallery
The Chinese Historical Society of America and Chinese American National
Museum, San Francisco

JAMES YEH-JAU LIU

Readings:

The Ark (Tiburon-Belvedere-Strawberry newspaper), August 19, 1987, July 23,
1997, July 26, 2000
Marin Independent Journal, June 2, 1991
The Paintings of James Yeh-jau Liu. April 1992

Awards/ Honors:

Citizen of the Year, 1987, Tiburon, California

Exhibitions:
Solo
Fine Arts Gallery of San Diego, California, 1972
National Museum of History, Taipei, Taiwan, 1985
City of Marysville, California, 1990, 1991, 1992, 1993, 1994, 1995
Butterfly House Gallery, Kobe, Japan, 1996
Gallery on the Rim, San Francisco, 1997, 1999
Tiburon Town Hall, Tiburon, California, 2000
Sun Yat-Sen Memorial Hall, San Francisco, 2000

Group
"Three Artists from Taiwan," San Francisco State University, 1962
"Three Artists," Lakey Gallery, Carmel, California, 1963
"Pacific Rim Exhibition," Salt Lake City, Utah, 1997
"Five Artists Who Influenced Art in California," Catherine Coffin Phillips Library,
Tiburon, California, 1998
"Artists From Three Locales," Chinese Arts Association, Millbrae, California,
1999
"Second Millennium Art Exhibition," Chinese Arts Association, Millbrae,
California, 2000

Collections:

Galtes Museum of the University of Santa Clara, Santa Clara, California
Angel Island Heritage Institute, Tiburon, California
City of Marysville, California
National Taiwan Arts Center, Taipei, Taiwan
National History Museum, Taipei, Taiwan

GEORGE MIYASAKI

Readings:

The Complete Printmaker, John Ross and Clare Romano, Collier McMillan,
London, 1972
Art in the San Francisco Bay Area , 1945-1980. Thomas Albright, University of
California Press, 1985
Views From Asian California 1920-1965. Michael D. Brown, 1992
George Miyasaki: The Early Prints. Stephen Wirtz Gallery, San Francisco, 1992
With New Eyes: Toward an Asian American Art History in the West. San
Francisco State University, 1995
A History of Lithography. Wilheim Weber, McGraw Hill, New York, 1996
The San Francisco School of Abstract Expressionism. Susan Landauer, University
of California Press, 1996
Asian Traditions/Modern Expressions. Abrams/ Rutgers University, 1997

Awards:

John Hay Whitney Opportunity Fellowship, 1957-1958
John Simon Guggenheim Foundation Fellowship, 1963-1964
Ford Foundation Purchase Prize, San Francisco Museum of Art, 1963
National Endowment for the Arts Artist's Fellowship, 1980-1981 and 1985-1986
Certificate of Merit, National Academy of Design, New York, 1995

Exhibitions:
Solo
Gumps Gallery, San Francisco, 1957
Worth Ryder Gallery, University of California, Berkeley, 1963
San Francisco Museum of Art, 1967
Stephen Wirtz Gallery, San Francisco, 1979
Portland Art Museum, Portland, Oregon, 1983
Paul Klein Gallery, Chicago, Illinois, 1989
Mary Ryan Gallery, New York, 1993

Group
Annual Painting and Print Exhibition, San Francisco Museum of Art, 1957
"American Prints Today" (traveling exhibition), 1959
100 Prints of the Year, Society of American Graphic Artists, New York, 1963
"Painters Behind Painters," California Palace of the Legion of Honor, San
Francisco, 1967
"Contemporary American Prints," Krannert Art Museum, Urbana, Illinois, 1970
"Photo/ Graphics," George Eastman House, Rochester, New York, 1971
"Bay Area 12: Monotypes/ Prints," Stephen Wirtz Gallery, San Francisco, 1978
"Abstract on Paper," Impressions Gallery, Boston, 1980
"Tamarind: A 25 Year Retrospective," Frederick S. Wight Art Gallery, University
of California at Los Angeles, 1984
"The Ethnic Idea: An Artistic Genesis," Berkeley Art Center, California, 1987
"Ten Years of Printmaking, Works from Magnolia Editions," California Museum of
Art, Santa Rosa, California, 1993
"With New Eyes: Toward an Asian American Art History in the West," Art
Department Gallery, San Francisco State University, 1995
"Asian Traditions/ Modern Expressions," Rutgers University (traveling) 1997-
1999

Collections:

Achenbach Foundation for Graphic Arts, Fine Arts Museums of San Francisco
Pasadena Art Museum
Library of Congress, Joseph Pennel Collection, Washington, D.C.
San Francisco Museum of Modern Art
Mills College, Oakland, California
Museum of Modern Art, New York
Art Institute of Chicago
Honolulu Academy of Arts
Boston Museum of Fine Arts
Metropolitan Museum of Art, New York
British Museum, London

JOHSEL NAMKUNG

Readings:

"The Art of Johsel Namkung." Herb Belanger, *The Seattle Times*, February 1973
"Photography and Music." Johsel Namkung, *Northwest Arts,* Vol. IV, No. 6, March 31, 1978
"Namkung Captures Spirit of Place." Deloris Tarzan, *The Seattle Times,* April 9, 1978
"Namkung the Naturalist." Thom Gunn, *Argus,* Vol. 85, No. 19, 1978
"Critique: Namkung Exhibit." Steve Schwartz, *Journal of Photography,* Council of Seattle Art Museum, No.1, 1978
"Discovering the Essence." James Burns, *Northwest Photography,* Vol. 3, No. 5, June 1980
"Natural Vision." Priscilla Turner, *Alaska Airlines Magazine,* July 1987
They Painted From Their Hearts: Pioneer Asian American Artists. Wing Luke Asian Museum, 1994
With New Eyes: Toward an Asian American Art History in the West. Art Department Gallery, San Francisco State University, 1995

Awards:

First Prize in singing, Third All Korea Music Contest, 1939
First Prize in singing, Ninth All Japan Music Concours, 1940

Exhibitions:
Solo
Henry Gallery, University of Washington, 1966, 1972, 1973
Reed College, Oregon, 1967
Seattle Art Museum, 1978
Foster/White Gallery, Washington, 1978, 1980, 1896
University of California, Santa Cruz, 1985
Shanghai Photographers Association, China, 1986

Group:
"Oriental Eye," Focus Gallery, San Francisco, 1973
Seattle Art Museum, 1977
The Washington Year, Henry Art Gallery, 1981
Pacific Northwest Artists and Japan,
The National Museum of Art, Osaka, Japan, 1982
One Hundred Years of Washington Photography:
Selected Artists, Tacoma Art Museum, 1989
"They Painted From Their Hearts, Pioneer Asian American Artists,"
Wing Luke Asian Museum, 1994
"With New Eyes: Toward an Asian American Art History in the West,"
Art Department Gallery, San Francisco State University, 1995
"Through Our Eyes: Twentieth Century Asian American Photography of the Pacific Northwest," Wing Luke Asian Museum, 2000
Tenth Annual Korean American Artists Association of Washington State Exhibition, Bank of America Gallery, 2000

Collections:

Seattle Art Museum
Oakland Museum
San Francisco Museum of Modern Art
Henry Art Gallery
SEA-Tac Airport, Seattle

ARTHUR OKAMURA

Readings:

Who's Who in America
Who's Who in the West
Who's Who in American Art
Who's Who Among Asian Americans
View From Asian California 1920-1965. Michael D. Brown, 1992
With New Eyes: Toward an Asian American Art History in the West.
San Francisco State University, 1995
Asian Traditions/ Modern Expressions, Abrams/ Rutgers University, 1997

Awards:

First Prize, Religious Arts, University of Chicago, 1953
Edward L. Reyerson Foreign Travel Fellowship, 1954
Neysa McMein Purchase Award, Whitney Museum of Art, 1960
Schwabacher-Frey Award, San Francisco Museum of Art, 1960
San Francisco Art Commission, Purchase Prize, 1976

Exhibitions:
Solo
Frank Ryan Gallery, Chicago, 1953
Feingarten Galleries, Chicago, New York, San Francisco, Los Angeles, 1956-1976
Santa Barbara Museum of Art, 1958
California Palace of the Legion of Honor, San Francisco, 1961
Hanson Gallery, San Francisco, 1964-1968
San Francisco Museum of Art, 1968
California College of Arts and Crafts, Oakland, 1972
Honolulu Academy of Arts, 1980
Ruth Braunstein Gallery, San Francisco, 1981, 1982, 1984, 1986, 1987, 1988, 1990, 1994
Recent Bolinas Landscapes, Commonweal, 20th Anniversary Celebration, Bolinas, California, 1996

Group
The Art Institute of Chicago Annuals, 1951, 1952, 1953, 1954
Downtown Gallery, New York, 1954
Contemporary Americans, Los Angeles County Museum, 1957
"Art in Asia and the West," San Francisco Museum of Art, 1957
"Fresh Paint," M.H. de Young Memorial Museum, San Francisco, 1958
Whitney Annual, 1962, 1963, 1964
Corcoran Gallery, Washington, D.C., 1964
"Painters Behind Painters," California Palace of the Legion of Honor, San Francisco, 1967
Asian Artists, Oakland Museum, 1971
Zen Gardens, San Jose State University, 1976
"A Sense of Place," Joslyn Art Museum, Nebraska, 1973
"Four from California College of Arts and Crafts," Berkeley Art Center, 1974
"Tropical Visions," St. Mary's College, 1989
"With New Eyes: Toward an Asian American Art History in the West,"
Art Department Gallery, San Francisco State University, 1995
"Asian Traditions/ Modern Expressions," Rutgers University, (traveling) 1997-1999

Film/ Television/ Set Design:

The Art of Pastel, Sharyle Patton, Director, 1977
Screen Printing, Magda Cregg Productions, 1978
The People, pastel drawings, television movie, John Korty, Director, 1971
Set Design: Watershed Environmental Poetry Festival, Band Shell, Golden Gate Park, San Francisco, 1997

Handmade Books:

1,2,3,4,5,6,7,8,9,0, with Robert Creeley, 1971
Basho, with Robert Bly, Mudra Publisher, 1972
10 Poems by Issa, with Robert Bly, Floating Island Publications, 1993
Magic Rabbit. Jungle Garden Press, 1995

Collections:

Rockefeller Chapel, University of Chicago
Art Institute of Chicago
Whitney Museum of Art
San Francisco Museum of Modern Art
Hirschhorn Museum
Achenbach Foundation for Graphic Arts, Fine Arts Museums of San Francisco
California Palace of the Legion of Honor, San Francisco
Smithsonian Institution
Stanford University
Oakland Art Museum

MINÉ OKUBO

Readings:

Citizen 13660. Miné Okubo, Columbia University Press, New York, 1946 and the University of Washington Press, 1973, 1983, 1989, 1991, 1994
Artists and People. Yvonne Greer Thiel, Philosophical Library, Inc., 1959
"Concentration Camp Boarders Strictly American Plan." New York Times Book Review, September 22, 1946
America's Concentration Camps. Allan Bosworth, W. W. Norton and Co., 1967
The View From Within: Japanese American Art From The Internment Camps 1942-1945. Karin M. Higa, Japanese American National Museum, Los Angeles, 1992, 1994
Miné Okubo: An American Experience, Commentary by Shirley Sun. Oakland Museum, 1972
Views From Asian California 1920-1965. Michael D. Brown, 1992
Contemporary American Success Stories: Famous People of Asian Ancestry. Vol. IV, Maryland Childs, Mitchell Lane Publishers, 1995
With New Eyes: Toward an Asian American Art History in the West. San Francisco State University, 1995

Awards/ Honors:

San Francisco Art Association Purchase Prize, 1937
Bertha Taussing Traveling Scholarship, University of California at Berkeley, 1938
Anonymous Donor Prize, San Francisco Museum of Art, 1940
Anne Bremer Prize, University of California Honor Society Art Show, 1940
San Francisco Museum Annual Prize, 1948
Selected one of 12 women pioneers in "The History of California 1800 to Present," California State Department of Education, 1987
Lifetime Contribution to the Visual Arts, Women's Caucus for Art, National Museum of Women, Washington, D.C., 1991
Lifetime Achievement Award, New York City, Celebration of Asian Pacific Island Heritage Month, 1998

Exhibitions:
Solo
San Francisco Museum of Art, 1940, 1941
Mortimer Levitt Gallery, New York, 1951
Image Gallery, Stockbridge, Massachusetts, 1968
"Miné Okubo: An American Experience," Oakland Museum, California, 1972
Riverside Junior College, 1974
Catherine Gallery, New York City, 1985
50 Year Retrospective, Japan Society of Boston, 1993

Group
National Traveling Exhibit of Paintings and Drawings of Japanese Relocation Camps, Common Council for American Unity, New York City, 1945
"As Nisei Saw It," Riverside Fine Arts Guild, Riverside Public Library, California, 1946
Paintings of Japanese Relocation Camps, California Historical Society, San Francisco, 1972
"The View from Within: Japanese American Art from the Internment Camps," 1942-1945, Japanese American National Museum, Los Angeles, (traveling) 1992-1994
"With New Eyes: Toward an Asian American Art History in the West," Art Department Gallery, San Francisco State University, 1995

Television:

"The Nisei: The Pride and the Shame," CBS TV News Feature, 1965

Collections:

Fine Arts Museums of San Francisco/ The Achenbach Foundation for Graphic Arts
The Oakland Museum
San Francisco Museum of Modern Art

TADASHI SATO

Readings:

Pacific Heritage (catalogue). Los Angles County Museum of Art, 1963
Artists of Hawaii: 19 Painters and Sculptors. Francis Haar And Prithwish Neogy, University Press of Hawaii, Honolulu, 1974
Paintings by Tadashi Sato. Honolulu Academy of Arts, 1985
"Sato Retrospective Traces 40 Year Evolution of Style." Joan Rose, Star-Bulletin and Advertiser, Honolulu, 1992
Asian Traditions/Modern Expressions. Abrams/ Rutgers University, 1997

Awards:

Brooklyn Museum Art School Scholarship, 1948
John Hay Whitney Opportunity Fellowship, 1954
Honolulu Community Foundation Scholarship, 1955
Albert Kapp Award, 1958

Exhibitions:
Solo
Gallery 75, New York
McRoberts and Tunnard Gallery, London
Richard White Gallery, Seattle
Contemporary Arts Center, Honolulu, 1963
Honolulu Academy of Arts, 1985
Hui No'eau Visual Arts Center, Kaluanui, Hawaii, 1992
Koa Gallery, Kapiolani Community College, April 2000

Group
"Young Painters of America," Guggenheim Museum, New York, 1952
"The Theater Collects American Art," Whitney Museum, 1961
"Pacific Heritage," Los Angeles County Museum of Art, 1963
Museum of Modern Art, New York
Albright Art Gallery, Buffalo, New York
M.H. de Young Memorial Museum, San Francisco
"Asian Traditions/Modern Expressions," Rutgers University, (traveling) 1997-1999

continued next page

Tadashi Sato continued

Collections:

Hawaii State Foundation on Culture and Arts,
Honolulu Academy of Arts
Guggenheim Museum, New York
Whitney Museum, New York

Public Murals:

War Memorial Center
Kahului Library, Maui
Aina Haina and Aiea Branch libraries, Oahu
Hawaii State Capitol
Honolulu Convention Center

KAY SEKIMACHI

Readings:

Beyond Craft: The Art Fabric. Mildred Constantine and Jack Lenor Larsen, Van Nostrand Reinhold Company, 1973
Fiber R/ Evolution. Milwaukee Art Museum, 1986
Fiber Concepts. Lucinda Gedeon, Arizona State University, 1989
New American Tapestry. Ruth Kaufman, Reinhold Book Corporation, 1968
"Kay Sekimachi: Successful On Her Own Terms."
Fiberarts, September/ October 1982
The Tactile Vessel, New Basket Forms. Erie Art Museum, Pennsylvania, 1989
L'Art Textile. Michel Thomas, Paris, Albert Skira, 1985
"Kay Sekimachi." Craft Horizons, May/ June, 1959
With New Eyes: Toward an Asian American Art History in the West. San Francisco State University, 1995
"Arts, Crafts and Marriage." Wall Street Journal, Wednesday. August 23, 1995

Awards/ Honors:

National Endowment for the Arts Fellowship, 1974
Fellow, American Craft Council, 1985

Exhibitions:
Solo/ 2 Person
Pacific Basin School of Textile Arts, Berkeley, California, 1974
"Side by Side: Kay Sekimachi and Bob Stocksdale," Contemporary Fine Art Gallery, Tokyo, Japan, 1985
"Intersections: Kay Sekimachi and Emily Dubois," Union Gallery, Purdue University, Indiana, 1991
"Forms of Grace, Kay Sekimachi and Bob Stocksdale," Beelke Gallery, Purdue University, Indiana, 1991
"Marriage in Form: Kay Sekimachi and Bob Stocksdale," Palo Alto Cultural Center, California, 1994

Group
Modern Wall Hangings, Victorian And Albert Museum, London, 1962-63
Wall Hangings, Museum of Modern Art, New York, 1968
"Deliberate Entanglements," University of California at Los Angeles, 1971
"Fiber As Art: Americas and Japan," National Museum of Modern Art, Kyoto and Tokyo, 1977-78
"Old Traditions/ New Directions," The Textile Museum, Washington, D.C., 1981
"The Art Fabric: Mainstream," San Francisco Museum of Art (traveling) 1981–83
"Japanese American Women Artists: Fiber and Metal," Evergreen State College, Olympia, Washington, 1984
"Fiber R/ Evolution," Milwaukee Art Museum, Wisconsin, 1986
"The Eloquent Object," Philbrook Museum of Art Center, Tulsa, Oklahoma, (traveling) 1987-1989

"Craft Today, USA," American Craft Museum, New York, 1986 (traveling in Europe, 1986-1993)
"Strength and Diversity: Japanese American Women 1985-1990," Oakland Museum, California, 1990
"Small Works in Fibers," The Mildred Constantine Collection, The Cleveland Museum of Art, Ohio, 1993
"With New Eyes: Toward an Asian American Art History in the West," Art Department Gallery, San Francisco State University, 1995
"Art After Incarceration," Pro Arts, Oakland, California, 1998

Collections

American Craft Museum, New York
Minneapolis Institute Of Arts, Minnesota,
Musee Des Arts Decoratifs, Paris, France
The Oakland Museum, California
Renwick Gallery of the National Museum of American Art, Smithsonian Institution, Washington, D.C.
National Museum of Modern Art, Kyoto, Japan
Royal Scottish Museum, Edinburgh, Scotland
Cleveland Museum of Art, Ohio

TSENG YUHO

Readings:

Some Contemporary Elements in Classical Chinese Painting. Tseng Yuho, University Press of Hawaii, 1963
Artists of Hawaii: 19 Painters and Sculptors. Francis Haar and Prithwish Neogy, University Press of Hawaii, 1974
Chinese Calligraphy. Philadelphia Museum of Art, 1971-72
Wenjen Hua (Literati Paintings). Honolulu Academy of Arts, 1988
Ten-Yi One. Contemporary Museum, Honolulu, 1989
"Innovations Follow Chinese Tradition." Marsha Morse, Sunday Star-Bulletin and Advertiser, Honolulu, July 30,1989.
"Tseng Yuho Restrospective, 1959-1989." Ronn Ronck, The Honolulu Advertiser, July 13, 1989
Dsui Hua/ Tseng Yuho. Hanart T Z Gallery, Taipei, 1992
The Living Brush: Four Masters of Contemporary Chinese Calligraphy. American Asian Cultural Exchange, San Francisco/ Pacific Heritage Museum, 1997
Asian Traditions/ Modern Expressions. Abrams/ Rutgers University, 1997
By Design: The Art of Tseng Yuho. Kaikodo Journal, New York, 2000

Awards/ Honors:

Louise Horowitz Scholarship, the Oriental Society, Washington, D.C., 1960
Los Angeles Book Association Award, book design for Some Contemporary Elements in Classical Chinese Painting, 1964
Fulbright Visiting Lectureship to Germany, 1966 -1967
New York University Foundation Day Honor Award, outstanding scholarship (Ph.D. thesis), 1972
"Living Treasure of Hawaii," Award for artistic contribution, 1990
"KOA Outstanding Artist" Award, 1998

Exhibitions:
Solo
Peking Union Medical College Hall, Beijing, China, 1946
M.H. de Young Memorial Museum, San Francisco, 1946-1947, 1953
Smithsonian Institution Traveling Exhibition (10 U.S. venues), 1955
Honolulu Academy of Arts Traveling Exhibition, 1959
The Downtown Gallery, New York, 1960, 1962
The Museum of Modern Art, New York (traveling), 1963
Honolulu Academy of Arts, 1989
National Museum of Contemporary Art, Shanghai, Beijing, Taipei, 1991
Art Center, Hong Kong, 1992
Singapore National Museum of Art, 1992
Hanart T Z Gallery, Taipei, 1992
KOA Gallery, Kapiolani Community College, Hawaii, 1998
Kaikodo, New York, 2000

Group

"Art of the Western States (Fresh Paint)," Stanford Art Gallery, Palo Alto,
California and M.H. de Young Memorial Museum, San Francisco, 1958
Downtown Gallery, New York, 1959-1972
American Painting and Sculpture, Art Festival, University of Illinois, 1958, 1960,
1962
Painting and Sculpture International, Carnegie Institute, Pittsburgh, Pennsylvania,
1965, 1968
"Impact of Nature," IBM Gallery, New York, 1965
Faculty Exhibitions, Art Department, University of Hawaii and Honolulu
Academy of Arts, 1969-1985
"Collective Vision, 30th Anniversary," State Foundation on Culture and the Arts,
Hawaii, 1997
"The Living Brush: Four Masters of Contemporary Chinese Calligraphy," Pacific
Heritage Museum, San Francisco, 1997
"Asian Traditions/ Modern Expressions," Rutgers University, New Jersey, (travel-
ing) 1997-1999
"Commitment to Excellence, 19thAnniversary,"The Honolulu Japanese Chamber
of Commerce, 1997

Stage Sets/ Murals:

Set for *Job*, Juilliard School of Music, New York, 1956
Mural, Golden West Savings and Loan Association, San Francisco, 1964
(destroyed)
12 Illustrations for "The Analects of Confucius" translation, Lionel Gile, The
Limited Edition Club, New York, 1967
Wall painting, Honolulu International Airport, 1973
Wall painting, Hilo Campus Center, Student Dining hall, University of Hawaii,
State Foundation on Culture and the Arts, 1979
Wall painting, Entrance Hall, BetWest, Inc., Honolulu, 1990

Film/ Video:

The Living Brush: Tseng Yuho. American Asian Cultural Exchange, San Francisco,
1997

Collections:

The Art Institute, Chicago
Museum fur Ostasiatische Kunst, Cologne, Germany
Honolulu Academy of Arts
Cornell University, Ithaca, New York
Milwaukee Art Center, Wisconsin
Museum of Eastern Art, Oxford, England
Musée Cernuschi, Paris, France
Stanford University, California
Marion Koogler McNay Art Institute, San Antonio, Texas, Munson Williams
Proctor Institute, Utica
Williams College, Williamstown, Massachusetts

GEORGE TSUTAKAWA

Readings:

"Fountains." *Art in America*, December 1964
Fountains in Contemporary Architecture. American Federation of the Arts, New
York, 1965
Art Treasures in the West. Sunset Magazine Publishers, Menlo Park, California,
1966
Art of the Pacific Northwest, from the 1930s to the Present. Smithsonian
Institution Press, Washington, D.C., 1974
George Tsutakawa and Morris Graves. Whitman College, Walla Walla,
Washington, 1978
Northwest Traditions. Martha Kingsbury, Seattle Art Museum and University of
Washington Press, 1978
Turning Shadows into Light: Art and Culture of the Northwest's Early Asian-
Pacific Community. Mayumi Tsutakawa and Alan Chong Lau, eds., Young Pine
Press, Seattle, 1982
George Tsutakawa. Martha Kingsbury, Bellevue Art Museum and University of
Washington Press, 1990
The Painted From Their Hearts: Pioneer Asian American Artists. Mayumi
Tsutakawa, ed., Wing Luke Asian Museum, 1994
With New Eyes: Toward an Asian American Art History in the West. San
Francisco State University, 1995
Asian Traditions/ Modern Expressions. Abrams/ Rutgers University Press, 1997

Awards/ Honors:

Washington State Governor's Award of Commendation, 1967
Order of Rising Sun Award, 4th Class, from Emperor of Japan, 1981
Washington State Historical Society's Centennial Hall of Honor Award, 1981
Alumnus Summa Laude Dignatus Award, University of Washington Alumni
Association, 1984
Honorary Lifetime Membership, American Institute of Architects, Seattle
Chapter, 1984
Honorary Doctorate of Fine Arts, Whitman College, Walla Walla, Washington,
1986

Exhibitions:
Solo
Studio Gallery, Seattle, 1947
Henry Gallery, University of Washington, Seattle, 1950, 1965
Altman Prechek Gallery, Bellevue, Washington, 1952
Seattle Art Museum, 1957
Summer Art Festival, Michigan State University, East Lansing, 1962
Kittredge Gallery, University of Puget Sound, Tacoma, Washington, 1964
Foster/ White Gallery, Seattle, 1978, 1981, 1984, 1988
Koko-Kan Museum, Sendai, Japan, 1981
PONCHO Gallery, Seattle Art Museum Pavilion, 1985
George Tsutakawa Retrospective, Bellevue Art Museum, Bellevue, Washington,
1990

Group
Art of the Pacific Northwest, National Collection of Fine Arts, Smithsonian
Institution, Washington, D.C. (traveling), 1974
"Northwest Traditions," Seattle Art Museum, 1978
George Tsutakawa and Morris Graves: Painting, Drawings and Sculpture, Olin
Gallery, Whitman College, Walla Walla, Washington, 1978
Pacific Northwest Artists and Japan, National Museum of Art, Osaka, Japan and
Seattle Art Museum, 1982
American Prints of the 1930s and 1940s, Seattle Art Museum, 1983
Seattle Style, *sumi-e* group show, touring exhibition in France, 1987-1988
Sumi Paintings, Bellevue Art Museum, Bellevue, Washington, 1988
Washington State Centennial Art Exhibition, Tacoma Art Museum, 1989
"The Painted From Their Hearts: Pioneer Asian American Artists," Wing Luke
Asian Museum, Seattle, 1994-95
"With New Eyes: Toward an Asian American Art History in the West," Art
Department Gallery, San Francisco State University, 1995
"Asian Traditions/ Modern Expressions," Rutgers University, New Jersey, (travel-
ing) 1997-1999

continued next page

George Tsutakawa continued

Fountains:

Fountain of Wisdom, Seattle Public Library, 1960
Fountain of Good Life, Commerce Tower, Kansas City, Missouri, 1964
Waiola Fountain, Ala Moana Center, Honolulu, Hawaii, 1966
Rain Fountain No. 2, Burien Library, Seattle, 1972
Fine Arts Court Fountain, Pennsylvania State University, University Park, 1974
Fountain of Joy, Setagaya Park, Tokyo, Japan, 1983
Lotus Fountain, Fukuyama Fine Art Museum, Fukuyama, Japan, 1988
Centennial Fountain, Central Plaza, Seattle University, Seattle, 1989

Collections:

Santa Barbara Museum of Art
Bellevue Arts and Crafts Association
Henry Gallery, University of Washington, Seattle
Seattle Art Museum
Seattle Public Library
Denver Art Museum

CARLOS VILLA

Readings:

"Carlos Villa." Walter Hopps, *Artforum*, September 1962
"The Dual Citizenship Art of Carlos Villa." Moira Roth, *Visions Art Quarterly*, Fall 1989
"The Art of Multicultural Weaving: Carlos Villa's Ritual." Moira Roth, *High Performance*, Fall 1989
"Carlos Villa at U.C. Davis." David S. Rubin, *Art in America*, Summer 1985
Mixed Blessings: New Art in a Multicultural America. Lucy R. Lippard, Pantheon Books, New York, 1990
"There Were No Filipino Art Books." Carlos Villa and DIWA artists, *Artweek*, July 4, 1991
Worlds in Collision: Dialogues Toward a Truer American Art History. Carlos Villa and Reagan Louie, eds., Austin and Winfield/ S.F. Art Institute, 1994
Carlos Villa. Moira Roth, Diane Tani, Mark Johnson, et. Al., eds., Visibility Press, Center for the Arts at Yerba Buena Gardens, Filipino American Arts Exposition and Philippine Resource Center, 1994
"O Her Blackness Sparkles" The Life and Times of the Batman Gallery 1960-1965. Jack Foley, 3300 Press, San Francisco, 1995
With New Eyes: Toward an Asian American Art History in the West. San Francisco State University, 1995

Awards/ Honors:

National Endowment for the Arts Grant, 1973
Adaline Kent Award, San Francisco Art Institute, 1974
Pollock-Krasner Award, New York, 1997
National Council of Art Administrators Award, 1999

Exhibitions:
Solo
Poindexter Gallery, New York, 1967
Richmond Art Center, Richmond, California, 1970
Hansen Fuller, San Francisco, 1970
University of San Diego with Joseph Raffael, 1971
Nancy Hoffman Gallery, New York, 1973, 1975
"A Painting Performance/ Interaction," The Farm, San Francisco, 1980
Helen Euphrat Gallery, De Anza College, Cupertino, California, 1980
Vorpal Gallery, San Francisco, 1981
San Francisco Museum of Modern Art, 1982
Retrospective, University of California at Davis, 1985

Janet Steinberg Gallery, San Francisco, 1987
Jennifer Pauls Gallery, San Jose, California, 1989
Pro Arts, Oakland, California, 1989
INTAR Gallery, New York, 1990
Mills College, Oakland, California, 1990
"Family Witnessing," Treganza Museum of Anthropology, San Francisco State University, 1998
Thatcher Gallery, University of San Francisco, 2000

Group
"Ratbastards," Spatsa Gallery, San Francisco, 1958
Fifteen Bay Area Artists, Poindexter Gallery, New York, 1961
Art of San Francisco, 90th Anniversary, San Francisco Art Institute, 1961
Bolles Gallery, San Francisco, 1962
Goldowsky Gallery, New York, c.1964
"Rhythms and Reverberations," M.H. de Young Memorial Museum, San Francisco, 1972
Whitney Annual, New York, 1972
"California Show: The Modern Era," San Francisco Museum of Modern Art and the National Collection of Fine Arts, Washington, D.C., 1976 – 1977
Havana Biennal, Cuba, 1989, 1991
International Hotel Installation, Center for the Arts at Yerba Buena Gardens, San Francisco, 1994
"With New Eyes: Toward an Asian American Art History in the West," Art Department Gallery, San Francisco State University, 1995
"Crossings: Fourteen Asian and Asian American Artists from the Bay Area," 101 California, San Francisco, 1998
"Freedom or Slavery, The Paul Robeson Portfolio," Alliance Press, Berkeley, California, (traveling) 1998-
"Mabuhay: Stories Old and New," Triton Museum, Santa Clara, California, 1999

Collections:

The Oakland Museum
E.B. Crocker Art Gallery, Sacramento, California
Richmond Art Center, Richmond, California
Smithsonian Institution, Washington, D.C.
Whitney Museum, New York
Columbia University, New York

C.C. WANG

Readings:

The Landscapes of C.C. Wang: Mountains of the Mind. Lois Katz and C.C. Wang, Arthur M. Sackler Foundation, New York, 1977
"Series of Interviews with C.C. Wang" by Hsu Hsiao-hu. *National Palace Museum Monthly*, Nos. 13-29, April 1984-August 1985.
C.C. Wang: Landscape Paintings. James Cahill, ed., University of Washington Press, 1987
The Living Brush: Four Masters of Contemporary Chinese Calligraphy. American Asian Cultural Exchange, San Francisco and Pacific Heritage Museum, 1997

Exhibitions:
Solo
M.H. de Young Memorial Museum, San Francisco, 1968
Retrospective Exhibition, Los Angeles County Museum of Art, 1971
China Institute in America, New York, 1972
Honolulu Academy of Arts, Hawaii, 1972
Indianapolis Museum of Art, 1972
Fogg Art Museum, Harvard University, Cambridge, Massachusetts, 1973
Chinese Culture Center, New York, 1973
Columbia University, New York, 1975
Chinese Culture Foundation, San Francisco, 1976
Retrospective, Brooklyn Museum, Brooklyn, New York, 1977

Hugh Moss Gallery, London, England, 1982
Hong Kong Arts Center, National Museum of History, Taipei, 1983
Retrospective "Mind Landscapes: The Paintings of C.C. Wang," Henry Art
Gallery, University of Washington, Seattle, and University of Kansas, 1988
The China Institute in America, New York, 1988
Taipei Fine Arts Museum, Taiwan, 1994
Plum Blossoms Gallery, Hong Kong and Singapore, 1994
"The C.C. Wang Family Collection of Fantastic Rocks" and "C.C. Wang: Old
Master, New Ideas," E. & J. Frankel Ltd., New York, 1995
Living Masters: Recent Paintings by C.C. Wang, Asian Art Museum, San Francisco,
1996

Group
Chinese Paintings at Mid-century, University of Chicago, 1971
Paintings and Calligraphy by Wu Hufan and His Students, Shanghai, 1981
Taipei Fine Arts Museum, Taipei, 1984
"The Mountain Retreat: Landscape in Modern Chinese Painting," Aspen Art
Museum, Colorado and Emily Lowe Gallery, Hofstra University, New York, 1986
"Six 20th Century Chinese Artists," from collection of Murray Smith, Los
Angeles County Museum of Art, 1989
Shenyang Museum, Liaoning, China, 1989
"Not Knowing: Affinities in Eastern and Western Art," Gallery Schlesinger, New
York, 1994
"The Living Brush: Four Masters of Contemporary Chinese Calligraphy," Pacific
Heritage Museum, San Francisco, 1997
"Asian Traditions/ Modern Expression," Rutgers University, (traveling) 1997-1999

Film/ Video:

The Living Brush: C.C. Wang. American Asian Cultural Exchange, San Francisco,
1997

Collections:

Art Museum, Princeton University, New Jersey
Brooklyn Museum, Brooklyn, New York
Fogg Art Museum, Harvard University
Metropolitan Museum of Art, New York
Asian Art Museum, San Francisco

ANNA WU WEAKLAND

Readings:

Anna Wu Weakland. Stanford University, California, 1988
Who's Who of American Women. 1995
With New Eyes: Toward an Asian American Art History in the West. San
Francisco State University, 1995

Awards/ Honors:

Lifetime Achievement Award, City of Palo Alto, California, 1996

Exhibitions:
Solo
M. H. de Young Memorial Museum, San Francisco, 1959
Hansen Galleries, San Francisco, 1960
La Jolla Art Museum, La Jolla, California, 1960
Pasadena Art Museum, California, 1962
Lanyon Gallery, Palo Alto, California, 1962
Seattle Art Museum, 1963
Ashmolean Museum, Oxford, England, 1964
Stanford University Art Gallery, 1965

Sale International/ Palacio De Bellas Artes, Mexico City, 1966
Downtown Gallery, New York, 1967
William Sawyer Gallery, San Francisco, 1969
Heritage Gallery, Los Angeles, 1971
Main Library, Palo Alto, California, 1975
Young-Sharin Gallery, Menlo Park, California, 1983
Palo Alto Medical Foundation, Palo Alto, California, 1984
Stanford University Art Museum, 1988

Group
Stanford University Art Museum, 1951
Hunter College, New York, 1953
Mills College, Oakland, California, 1958
Gump's Gallery, San Francisco, 1960
"With New Eyes: Toward an Asian American Art History in the West," Art
Department Gallery, San Francisco State University, 1995

Collections:

Ashmolean Museum, Oxford, England
Sale International/ Palacio De Bellas Artes, Mexico City
University of British Columbia, Vancouver, Canada
Greater Victoria Art Museum, Victoria, Canada
IBM Corporation
Seattle Art Museum
Stanford University
Mental Research Institute, Palo Alto, California

CHARLES WONG

Readings:

"The Year of the Dragon." *San Francisco Chronicle*, October 1st and 2nd, 1952
"The Year of the Dragon." Aperture Vol. 2, No. 1, 1952
"The Work of Sixteen Contemporary Photographers," U.S. Camera Yearbook,
1956

Awards/ Honors:

Northern California Art Scholarship to the California School of Fine Arts, 1939
3rd Honorable Mention, *Life Magazine* Photography Contest, 1951
Albert Bender Award in Photography, California School of Fine Arts, 1951-1952

Exhibitions:
Solo
"Camera in Hand," George Eastman House, Rochester, New York, 1956

Group
"The Discovery Show" San Francisco Museum of Art and George Eastman
House, Rochester, New York, c. 1951-1952
"The Scale," San Francisco Museum of Art, 1952

Radio:

"Year of the Dragon," KCBS Radio feature, San Francisco, June 13, 1952

Collections:

Anne Bremer Memorial Library, San Francisco Art Institute, San Francisco
George Eastman House, Rochester, New York,

JADE SNOW WONG

Readings:

"Potter in Person, Jade Wong Creates While the World Looks on Through a Glass Window." Phyllis Liapes, *San Francisco Newspaper*, December 1945
Fifth Chinese Daughter. Jade Snow Wong, Harper and Row, New York, 1950 and University of Washington Press, 1989, 1990, 1991, 1993
Photographic feature, *National Geographic*, October, 1956
The Immigrant Experience: The Anguish of Becoming American. Dial Press, New York, 1971 and Reissued, Penguin Press
No Chinese Stranger. Jade Snow Wong, Harper and Row, New York, 1975
Unbound Feet: A Social History of Chinese Women in San Francisco. Judy Yung, University of California Press, 1995
With New Eyes: Toward an Asian American Art History in the West. San Francisco State University, 1995
Who's Who in the West, c.1950's, 1960's
International Authors and Writers Who's Who, c.1950's, 1960's

Awards/ Honors:

California State Fair (for pottery), 1947
California State Fair (for enamels), 1949
Craftsmanship Silver Medal, *Mademoiselle Magazine,* 1948
Woman Warrior Award for Outstanding Contribution in Literature and Service
Distinguished Service/Cultural Award, Chinese Culture Center, San Francisco
Pioneer Award, Asian American Teachers Association
Honorary Doctor of Humane Letters, Mills College, California, 1976

Exhibitions:
Solo
North Texas Teachers College, Denton, Texas, 1949
Portland Art Museum, Oregon, 1951
Kansas City Art Institute and School of Design, Kansas City, Missouri, 1952
Joselyn Memorial Museum, Omaha, Nebraska, 1952
Detroit Institute of Arts, 1952
Chicago Art Institute, 1952
Traveling Exhibition, U.S. Information Service: Singapore, Kuala Lumpur, Penang Rangoon, Calcutta, Delhi, Karachi, c. Mid-50s.

Group
National Ceramic Exhibitions, Syracuse Museum of Fine Arts, 1947, 1948, 1949, 1950, 1951
Museum of Modern Art, New York, 1947
Cornell University, Ithaca, New York, 1948
American Craftsmen's Educational Council, New York, 1948
California State Fairs, Sacramento, California, c. 1950 – 1960
Cincinnati Art Museum
Denver Art Museum
M.H. de Young Memorial Museum, San Francisco
Merchandise Mart of Chicago, 1950
Mills College Art Gallery, Oakland, California
Oakland Museum
San Francisco Museum of Art
Smithsonian Institution: National Collection of Fine Arts
Washington University, St. Louis
Chinese Culture Center, San Francisco

Film:

PBS Adaptation of Fifth Chinese Daughter for the 1976 U.S. Bicentennial. Awarded best educational feature 1977, American Film Festival, New York

Collections:

Detroit Institute of Arts
Florida State University
International Ceramic Museum, Faenza, Italy
Joselyn Memorial Museum, Omaha, Nebraska
Metropolitan Museum of Art, New York
Oakland Museum, California
Mills College, Oakland, California

NANYING STELLA WONG

Readings:

International Who's Who in Poetry, c.1970's
Ting The Cauldron: Chinese Art and Identity in San Francisco. Glide Urban Center, San Francisco, 1970
An Anthology of World Poets. Henry, Bern Porter, Publisher, San Francisco and New York, 1970
Peace and Pieces: An Anthology of Contemporary American Poetry. 1973
Who's Who of American Women. 1975, 1976, 1977 1978
World Poetry. 1985
Views From Asian California 1920-1965. Michael D. Brown, 1992
Bearing Dreams, Shaping Visions, Asian Pacific American Perspectives. University of Washington Press, 1993
With New Eyes: Toward an Asian American Art History in the West. San Francisco State University, 1995

Awards/ Honors:

Bay Area Art Lovers Association Honored Artist Award, 1941
Margaret Shedd Writer's Award to study in Mexico City, 1951
Grand Prize, Contra Costa International Poetry Contest, for poem "Angel Island," 1977
Who's Who in Poetry Certificate of Merit, Cambridge, England, 1977
California Art Council Grant, Artist in Residence, Vista College, 1972-1982
Lifetime Achievement Award for Contribution to the Arts, Chinese Historical Society of America, San Francisco, 2000

Exhibitions:
Solo
Gump's Gallery, San Francisco, c.1940s
Paul Elder's, San Francisco, 1940
Berkeley City Club, Berkeley, California, 1961
Kahn's Rotunda Gallery, Oakland, California, pre-1960s
Zellerbach Playhouse, University of California at Berkeley, c.1960s-early 1970s
Pacific Association of the Arts Gallery, El Cerrito, California, 1969-1970
East/ West Exhibition, Oakland Museum, California, 1973
Association for Asian American Studies, Asian Resource Center, Oakland, California, 1995

Group
Oakland Museum, California, c.1932 – 35
Chinese Art Association, M.H. de Young Memorial Museum, San Francisco, 1935
Golden Gate International Exhibition: Contemporary Masters, Treasure Island, San Francisco, 1939
Berkeley Art Center, California, c. 1960s-1970s
Piezo Electric Gallery, (with son Colin), New York, 1987
"With New Eyes: Toward an Asian American Art History in the West," Art Department Gallery, San Francisco State University, 1995

Collections:

Private

TYRUS WONG

Readings:

"Art and Artist." Kenneth Rose, *Pasadena Star News*, February 23, 1947
Kitelines, Summer-Fall, 1983, Vol. 4, No. 4
Bambi: The Story and the Film. Frank Thomas and Ollie Johnston, Stewart, Tabori And Chang, New York, 1990
On Gold Mountain: The One Hundred Year Odyssey of My Chinese American Family. Lisa See, Vintage Books, 1995
Before the Animation Begins: The Art and Lives of Disney Inspirational Sketch Artists. John Canemaker, Hyperion, New York, 1996
Walt Disney's Bambi: The Sketchbook Series. Frank Thomas and Ollie Johnston, eds., Applewood Books, Hyperion, New York, 1997
"Drawing on the Wind," *Los Angeles Times Magazine*, May 23, 1999

Awards/ Honors:

Huntington Assistance Prize, Otis Institute of Art, 1935
Los Angeles Art Association, Los Angeles County Museum of Art Award for Watercolor, 1954
Butler Institute of American Art Award, c.1950s
American Watercolor Society's Kudner Prize for Watercolor, 1960

Exhibitions:
Solo
Pasadena Art Institute, 1947

Group (all c.1940s-1960s except as noted)
Library of Congress
Pennsylvania Academy of Fine Art
Santa Barbara Museum of Art
Denver Art Museum
Brooklyn Museum
San Francisco Museum of Art
Los Angeles County Art Museum, 1954
Butler Institute of American Art
Honolulu Academy of Arts
Charles and Emma Frye Art Museum, Seattle, Washington, 1960
On Gold Mountain, Autry Museum of Western Heritage, Los Angeles, 2000-2001

Film/ Inspirational Sketches and Storyboards:

Bambi. Walt Disney, 1942
The Sands of Iwo Jima. 1949
The Fighting Kentuckian. 1949
Around the World in 80 Days. 1956
Ice Palace. 1960
Harper. 1966
The Wild Bunch. 1969

Collections:

Santa Barbara Museum of Art
Los Angeles County Museum of Art
Butler Institute of American Art
Bowdoin College
Honolulu Academy of Arts
American Watercolor Society

Interviews were conducted by Irene Poon (Andersen) with the following artists:

Dong Kingman, New York City, New York, 1996 with the assistance of Stan Andersen (SPA)
Bernice Bing, Philo, California, 1997
Anna Wu Weakland, Palo Alto, California, 1997
Jade Snow Wong, San Francisco, California, 1997
Nanying Stella Wong, Berkeley, California, 1997
Tseng Yuho, Honolulu, Hawaii, 1997 (written interview)
Wah Ming Chang, Carmel, California, 1998
Benjamen Chinn, San Francisco, California, 1998
Taneyuki Dan Harada, Berkeley, California, 1998
Dale Joe, New York City, New York, 1998
George Miyasaki, Berkeley, California, 1998
Arthur Okamura, Bolinas, California, 1998
Charles Wong, San Francisco, California, 1999

AN OPEN LETTER:
Why sponsor an Asian American Art Show at a Christian College?

Dear Readers,

I am grateful for the opportunity to fund the art exhibition and concurrent catalogue, "Leading The Way: Asian American Artists of the Older Generation" at Gordon College. I come from a family with a heritage in business, literature, art, music, Christianity and charitable giving. A few years ago I was looking for a way to help the students at my alma mater, Gordon College, become better-equipped leaders for an increasingly pluralistic world. I decided that art would be a very effective tool for enhancing cross cultural understanding and appreciation.

I enlisted the help of fellow Christians, So Kam Lee, Asian art historian; Irene Poon, an artist in her own right, who has been documenting the work and biographies of Asian American artists; and Craig Ing, a graphic designer. I also approached Gordon College with the idea of this project. After a few years of hard work and prayer, I am now more convinced than ever that this is a perfect gift from a group of Christians to America at the beginning of this new millennium.

From the time of the Puritans arrival, Christianity has been an integral part of mainstream American culture. However, in the closing decades of the last century, conservative Christians seem to find themselves increasingly at odds with the American art world and mainstream popular culture. By providing this platform for an under represented group of accomplished artists, this project affirms that evangelical Christians support the freedom of expression of all Americans. It also recognizes the creative impulse reflective of our Creator.

Christians believe immorality is common in all humanity because of the Fall in Eden. At the same time, we believe that all humanity, is created in the image of God. Therefore, we must be bold in speaking out against evil; but we must respect the right of others to disagree with us. More importantly, Christians need to embrace any art or aspect of human culture that is good, wholesome and creative. These are the very qualities Christians believe can be found in all humanity, reflecting the very image of God. This project points to a common ground between East and West celebrating all art that is excellent, beautiful and wholesome. It is my hope and prayer that this project will lead to a more positive and balanced cultural dialogue as we engage one another in this new millennium.

Please enjoy this gift from both my biological and spiritual families to you!

Rev. Philip S. Lee
Gordon College, Class of 1982.